SECOND EDITION

Learning-Focused Supervision

Developing Professional Expertise in Standards-Driven Systems

Laura Lipton   Bruce Wellman

Solution Tree | Press

Copyright © 2025 by Laura Lipton and Bruce Wellman

All rights reserved, including the right of reproduction of this book in whole or in part in any form.

555 North Morton Street
Bloomington, IN 47404
800.733.6786 (toll free) / 812.336.7700
FAX: 812.336.7790

email: info@SolutionTree.com
SolutionTree.com

Visit **go.SolutionTree.com/leadership** to download the free reproducibles for this book.

Printed in the United States of America

Library of Congress Cataloging-in-Publication Data

Names: Lipton, Laura, author. | Wellman, Bruce M., author.
Title: Learning-focused supervision : developing professional expertise in
  standards-driven systems / by Laura Lipton and Bruce Wellman.
Description: Second edition. | Bloomington, IN : Solution Tree Press,
  [2024] | Includes bibliographical references and index.
Identifiers: LCCN 2024027088 (print) | LCCN 2024027089 (ebook) | ISBN
  9781962188432 (softcover) | ISBN 9781962188449 (ebook)
Subjects: LCSH: Teaching. | School supervision. | Educational change. |
  Education--Philosophy. | Teams in the workplace. | Educational
  evaluation. | School improvement programs.
Classification: LCC LB1025 .L57 2024 (print) | LCC LB1025 (ebook) | DDC
  371.2/03--dc23/eng/20240716
LC record available at https://lccn.loc.gov/2024027088
LC ebook record available at https://lccn.loc.gov/2024027089

Solution Tree
Jeffrey C. Jones, CEO
Edmund M. Ackerman, President

Solution Tree Press
President and Publisher: Douglas M. Rife
Associate Publishers: Todd Brakke and Kendra Slayton
Editorial Director: Laurel Hecker
Art Director: Rian Anderson
Copy Chief: Jessi Finn
Acquisitions Editors: Carol Collins and Hilary Goff
Content Development Specialist: Amy Rubenstein
Associate Editors: Sarah Ludwig and Elijah Oates
Editorial Assistant: Anne Marie Watkins

Originally published by MiraVia, LLC.

Acknowledgments

This work emerges from our long-term curiosity about ways to create learning-focused relationships between supportive colleagues. In our quest to discover, refine, and teach the dispositions and skills of this craft, we have had our own enriching learning relationships with our many clients and colleagues across the U.S. and Canada, as well as internationally.

We are especially indebted to our MiraVia training associates for their insights, questions, and feedback which continues to push our thinking. Much thanks to Lisa Danielson, Pati Falk, Barbara Lawson, Peggy Olcott, and Lynn Sawyer for these efforts.

This book would not have been possible without the keen eye and language skills of our editor, Karen Boss and the graphic skills and craftsmanship of our designer and compositor Rebecca Manchester.

And thank you as always to June Lipton, our media master.

> "At the highest levels of expert performance, the drive for improvement will always involve search and experimentation at the threshold of understanding, even for the masters dedicated to redefining the meaning of excellence in their fields."
> – Anders Ericsson

Contents

Introduction		xi
SECTION 1	**Learning-Focused Supervision in Action**	1-10
	Assumptions Informing Learning-Focused Supervision	1
	Embracing the Identity of a Learning-Focused Supervisor	3
	Dispositions	3
	Skills	4
	Technical Knowledge	5
	Four Qualities of Learning-Focused Supervision	5
	Comparing Supervisory Approaches	5
	Four Qualities	6
	Interaction Patterns Among Qualities	9
SECTION 2	**Four Stances: The Continuum of Learning-Focused Interaction**	11-40
	Three Supervisory Competencies: Fluency, Flexibility, and Fluidity	12
	Fluency	12
	Flexibility	12
	Fluidity	12
	The Four Stances	13
	Calibrating	13
	Consulting	17
	Collaborating	21
	Coaching	24
	Cueing Stance	26
	Navigating Strategically	28
	Adjusting Stance	28
	Six Supervisor Strategies When Navigating the Continuum of Learning-Focused Interaction	29
	Focusing the Conversation: Establishing the Third Point	31
	Mediating Nonverbally	32
	Customized Conversations	33
	The Intersection of Attitude and Aptitude	33
	Quadrant I	34
	Quadrant II	35
	Quadrant III	36
	Quadrant IV	37
	Versatility Matters	38

Contents *(continued)*

SECTION 3	**Structured Conversations**	**41-54**

Planning Conversations. 43
    Specialized Planning: Goal-Setting Conversations . . 47
Reflecting Conversations 48
Problem-Solving Conversations. 49
Navigating Within and Across the Conversation Templates 51
Integrating the Conversation Templates and the
Continuum of Learning-Focused Interaction 51
Learning-Focused Conversations: The Importance
of Structure 53

SECTION 4	**A Learning-Focused Tool Kit**	**55-86**

The Habit Cycle 57
Attending Fully. 58
    Communicating Attention 59
    Attunement and Alignment. 60
Listening to Understand 60
    Four Blocks to Understanding 61
    Listening and the Habit Cycle 62
Pacing for Thoughtfulness: Using Purposeful Pauses . . . 63
    Purposeful Pausing. 64
    Pausing as a Habit 64
Applying Verbal Tools 65
Entering the Teacher's World: Using Paraphrase. 65
    Three Types of Paraphrases with Three Intentions . . . 66
    Paraphrase as a Habit 68
    Paraphrase and Problem-Solving 68
    Well-Formed Goal Paraphrases. 69
    Shifting Language, Shifting Thought:
    Levels of Abstraction 71
Invitational Inquiry 72
    Designing Questions to Promote Thinking 73
    Creating the Conditions for Thinking 74
    Template for Inquiry 74
    The Invitation 74
    Cognition: Stimulating and Clarifying Thinking . . . 77
    Intention-Driven Questions: Inquiry to Clarify Thinking 78
    Deletions and Generalizations 79
    Generalizations 81

Contents (continued)

    Directing the Inquiry: The Topic 83
    Developmental and Customized Inquiries 84
    Increasing the Impact of Inquiries:
    Description to Thoughtfulness 84
    Invitational Inquiry as a Habit 85
    Developing Fluency with the
    Learning-Focused Tool Kit 85

SECTION 5 **Data as a Tool for Growth** 87-100
  Data and Standards 87
  Avoiding Bias: The Importance of Low-Inference Data . . 88
    Strategies for Avoiding Bias 89
  Choosing Data to Ensure Relevancy 90
    Avoiding Overload: Sharing the Data 90
    Applying Data in Learning-Focused Conversations . . 91
    Using Data in Each Stance of the Continuum of
    Learning-Focused Interaction 91
    Data as a Third Point 92
  Getting Started with Data 93
    Types of Data 93
  Using Data in Structured Conversations 95
    Clarifying Goals: The Planning Conversation 95
    Data and Inquiries: The Reflecting Conversation . . . 96
    Searching for Solution:
    The Problem-Solving Conversation 97
    Data-Based Discoveries During
    Learning-Focused Conversations 98
    Four Qualities of Learning-Focused
    Supervision in Action 98

SECTION 6 **From Novice to Expert Teaching** 101-126
  Two Types of Expertise: Routine and Adaptive 101
    Adaptive Expertise in Teaching 102
  Five Spheres of Teaching Expertise 103
    Knowledge of the Structure of the Discipline 104
    Knowledge of Teaching Skills and Strategies 106
    Knowledge of Learners and Learning 108
    Knowledge of Self 110
    Knowledge of Collaboration 111
  The Transition from Novice to More Expert Teaching . . 113

Contents (continued)

        The Inner Voice of Expertise 113
        Five Stages of Growth 114
    Five Stages of Growth .115
        Novice 115
        Advanced Beginner 115
        Competent 115
        Proficient 115
        Expert 115
    Supervision Across Developmental Stages 116
    Developmental Practice: Seven Lenses for Listening . . .116
        The Depth of Content Knowledge 118
        The Source of Goals for Lessons and Units 119
        Instructional Design and Delivery 120
        The Ability to Recognize and Generate Choice Points .121
        Depth of Evidence Cited 122
        Approaches to Problem-Solving 123
        Relationship to Professional Community 124
        Supervisory Expertise That
        Supports Teaching Expertise 125

References 127-130
Index 131-134
About the Authors 135

Tables

Table 1.1	Comparing Supervisory Approaches	5
Table 1.2	Developmental Qualities	6
Table 1.3	Standards-Driven Qualities	7
Table 1.4	Data-Based Qualities	8
Table 1.5	Customized Qualities	9
Table 2.1	Supervisor Strategies When Calibrating	16
Table 2.2	Supervisor Strategies When Consulting	18-20
Table 2.3	Supervisor Strategies When Collaborating	23
Table 2.4	Supervisor Strategies When Coaching	25
Table 2.5	The Continuum of Learning-Focused Interaction	27
Table 2.6	Adjusting Stance	28-29
Table 2.7	Six Supervisor Strategies When Navigating the Continuum of Learning-Focused Interaction	29-30
Table 2.8	Supervisor Strategies for Quadrant I Teachers	35

Tables (continued)

Table 2.9	Supervisor Strategies for Quadrant II Teachers	36
Table 2.10	Supervisor Strategies for Quadrant III Teachers	37
Table 2.11	Supervisor Strategies for Quadrant IV Teachers	38
Table 4.1	Supervisor Strategies with the Learning-Focused Tool Kit	56
Table 4.2	Clarifying Vague Language	82
Table 4.3	Developmental Inquiries	84
Table 4.4	From Description to Thoughtfulness	85
Table 5.1	Using Data with The Continuum of Learning-Focused Interaction	92
Table 5.2	Examples of Quantitative and Qualitative Data	94
Table 6.1	Seven Lenses for Listening	117
Table 6.2	Supervisor Strategies for Developing Depth of Content Knowledge	118
Table 6.3	Supervisor Strategies for Developing the Source of Goals for Lessons and Units	119
Table 6.4	Supervisor Strategies for Developing Instructional Design and Delivery	120
Table 6.5	Supervisor Strategies for Developing Ability to Recognize and Generate Choice Points	121
Table 6.6	Supervisor Strategies for Developing Depth of Evidence Cited	122
Table 6.7	Supervisor Strategies for Developing Approaches to Problem-Solving	123
Table 6.8	Supervisor Strategies for Developing Relationship to Professional Community	124

Figures

Figure 1.1	Four Qualities of Learning-Focused Supervision	6
Figure 2.1	Continuum of Learning-Focused Interaction	11
Figure 2.2	The Intersection of Attitude and Aptitude	34
Figure 3.1	Learning-Focused Conversations: A Template for Planning	44
Figure 3.2	Learning-Focused Conversations: A Template for Reflecting	45
Figure 3.3	Learning-Focused Conversations: A Template for Problem-Solving	46
Figure 4.1	Learning-Focused Tool Kit	55
Figure 4.2	The Habit Cycle/Breaking the Habit Cycle	57
Figure 4.3	The Components of Inquiry	74
Figure 4.4	Invitational Inquiry Exercise Mat	86

Figure 6.1   Five Spheres of Teaching Expertise 103
Figure 6.2   Pedagogical Content Knowledge 107

Downloadable Resources and Exercises

Visit **go.SolutionTree.com/leadership** to access the following tools.

Assessment Inventories

    Form A: Learning-Focused Supervision Primary Traits Self-Assessment

    Form B: Effective Listening Survey

Video Skill Development Exercises

    Form C: Video Exercise Paraphrase

    Form D: Video Exercise Inquiry: The Invitation

    Form E: Video Exercise Inquiry: Clarifying Vague Language

    Form F: Video Exercise Learn by Viewing: Processing a Learning-Focused Conversation Model

    Form G: Video Exercise: Types of Paraphrase

Learning Resources

    Invitational Inquiry Mat

Types of Paraphrase
vimeo.com/miravia/paraphrasing

Introduction:
Supervision in Flux

Instructional supervision is at a critical juncture. Entrenched customs, infrequent teacher observations, and feel-good feedback will not stimulate the vital forms of instructional improvement and teacher growth that schools need.

The context within and around schools is steadily shifting. Impossible to predict events are pressuring teachers and school leaders to adapt and upgrade their knowledge, skills, and practices as an ongoing condition of professional life. Thoughtful supervisors are navigating the tensions of balancing mandated evaluation functions with the need for relational trust and emotional support, to encourage teachers' continual learning and growth.

A related issue is the need to develop a shared vision and agreement within schools and districts about the observable characteristics of good teaching as defined by teaching standards and related rubrics. The underlying goal is to build a standards-based culture of learning for the adults in schools, so teachers can build a standards-based culture of learning in their classrooms. Just as teachers need to agree with what defines a "four" on a rubric that measures some aspect of student learning, teachers and supervisors need to develop common ground about what defines a "four" on specific aspects of teaching performance.

The focus of the supervisory process is shifting from fulfilling contractual obligations to promoting opportunities for growth, from using data to prove to using data to improve, from evaluation as an event to evaluation as a process, and from teachers asking, "What are my scores?" to asking, "What are my goals?"

This transition requires both cognitive and affective attention to the supervisory relationship. Clear intentions, conveyed through standards-based conversations that communicate high expectations and care for teachers' emotional well-being, promote high expectations for both staff and students.

Much of the impetus for these initiatives stems from two related concepts: that teacher effectiveness links directly to student learning, and that skillful supervision links directly to teacher effectiveness.

High-quality evaluation systems require three essential components: 1) clearly articulated and well understood standards with associated performance scales; 2) high levels of supervisor observation and analysis skills to support the framing of consistent evidence-based judgments; and 3) both formative and summative conferences aimed at teacher development rather than remediation.

Studies suggest that the first two components alone are insufficient for motivating teacher skill development and changes in practice without the third component in place. The supervisor's confidence and competence with conducting learning-focused conferences make the fundamental difference in teacher growth (Sartain et al., 2011; Kraft & Christian, 2019).

Thus, for supervisors, the ability to structure and facilitate powerful learning-focused conversations lies at the heart of both one-to-one and collective work with teachers. Standards provide the what (to talk about) and learning-focused supervision offers the how.

This book's content is centered around this idea: structuring conversations about what powerful student learning looks like and the ways teachers support and energize learning is the essential role of supervisors. Engaging in rich exchanges in one-to-one settings and with teams and departments increases both personal and collective efficacy—the conviction that teachers can make a difference for their students and overcome obstacles to learning. These beliefs lead to the following three premises.

1. Quality teaching matters for successful student learning. All learners, especially the most vulnerable, need highly skilled teachers.

2. Effective teaching can be measured and described by clearly articulated standards that are based on scales and expressed in rubrics.

3. Skillful supervision, focused by data-based conferencing skills and timely feedback, motivates and sustains teacher learning and growth.

Expanded Goals for Equity and Excellence

Expanding expectations for the type of learning students need to thrive in a rapidly changing world drives the push for new classroom practices in instruction, assessment, and student feedback (Darling-Hammond & Oakes, 2019). There is ongoing rethinking about what the essential curriculum is for these times, including a push to incorporate technological innovations.

The awareness that greater educational equity among students of different races and across socioeconomic strata comes with an increased focus on achievement gaps among and within schools. Add to that the importance of addressing student social-emotional needs and addressing the traumas that students bring to school from their homes and communities. All these considerations require new forms of pedagogy, which in turn require new forms of teacher learning, that further require new forms of teacher support and new forms of teacher supervision.

As part of this work, a related supervisory challenge is to significantly reduce within-school variations in student performance. This is to move beyond the celebration of a few shining stars, and instead ignite a culture wherein good ideas and effective practices spread and become normal rather than exceptional. There are dramatic differences in the amount of higher-level content and higher-level thinking that students experience in neighboring classrooms. These variances in instructional quality are often greater from classroom to classroom within schools than the variances among schools. Islands of distinguished practice are not enough to produce rich learning for all learners (Rothman, 2009).

In-depth classroom observations have found little evidence that inconsistencies emerge from teachers' responses to perceived student needs and that neither students' socioeconomic background nor prior achievement levels predict whether teachers emphasize a particular topic, skill, or cognitive demands of a given task. Many of the vast differences in teaching practices are related to a lack of clear standards for instruction on the teacher's part. Without clear and agreed-upon definitions of effective practice, teachers are left to themselves to define good teaching (Merseth et al., 2009).

Changing Student Demographics

Significant change in student demographics is a key factor driving the need for transformations in both teaching and supervisory practices. The current decline in the white student population is projected to continue until at least the fall of 2027, as is the percentage of Black students. The percentages of Hispanic, Asian, and biracial or multiracial students are projected to continue to increase (National Center for Education Statistics, Fast Facts).

Compounding the challenges of racial and ethnic diversity are two related elements: an increase in English Language Learners (ELLs) and the troubling number of American students living in poverty. Each of these factors brings staffing concerns and the need for expanded teacher training and increased supervisory flexibility (National Center for Education Statistics, Conditions, 2018).

Gray, Green, and White: Trends in the Teaching Force

While student demographics are transforming schools, the teaching force is undergoing dramatic fluctuations as well. Four factors that have major implications for the work of instructional supervisors are shaping these shifts: 1) an aging teaching force; 2) a surge of beginning teachers as the teaching force has grown, including recent college graduates and older career switchers; 3) a growing percentage of teachers who are white women; and 4) the wave of exits from the profession due to fatigue, stress, and understaffing leading to burdening professional responsibilities.

The racial composition of the teaching population remains a major concern for policy makers and practitioners. While the number of public school teachers who are BIPOC has more than doubled since the late 1980s to total around 762,000 in 2016, the teaching force still looks less and less like the students in our schools.

The other troubling trend in the teacher-demographic story is a dramatic increase in teacher turnover. High-poverty, high-minority, urban, and rural schools have highest rates of staff departures, with teachers of color having significantly higher rates than white teachers. Some of this movement is created by teachers leaving one school for another, while some depart for personal or family reasons, and many abandon the profession all-together (Ingersoll et al., 2018).

In addition, external conditions produce uncertainty and chaos in schools and put pressure on supervisors to maintain high academic standards while being sensitive to the social-emotional needs of staff and students.

Given the demographic, sociological, public health, and political forces interacting inside and outside of schools, the capabilities of instructional leaders to shape and manage school life are vitally important to develop and support (Klinger, 2020).

Learning-Focused Supervision

It has become resoundingly clear that educators are called upon to be responsive in times of extraordinary uncertainty. The emotional stress, anxiety, depression, and fear this ambiguity brings require teachers to be flexible and adaptable in their approach to supporting students across a wide range of needs. As a result, it is critical that supervisors can do the same for teachers. The ability to pivot nimbly to support a school's academic, social-emotional, and custodial functions demands that leaders be flexible, innovative, and other-minded (Edmondson, 2020).

Learning-focused supervision is a model for developing teachers' professional expertise that shifts school culture toward collaborative engagement in standards-based systems. This approach to supervision presents a skill set for increasing communication flexibility, promoting awareness of potential bias, and developing the capacity of others to learn and grow.

Inside this Book

Learning-Focused Supervision: Developing Professional Expertise in Standards-Driven Systems is a practical learning guide for instructional supervisors at all levels of experience. Feedback from users of the earlier edition, from our own work, and from the work of our training associates has greatly influenced this new edition.

Readers will find focusing questions at the start of each section, illustrations of supervisor/teacher interactions, and examples of specific supervisor strategies for each of the central concepts presented in this book. Also included are "Expert Moves" to guide practice and "Implications & Applications" for integrating and enhancing supervisory skills. QR codes with links to video clips that illustrate essential skills and processes are embedded throughout.

This second edition expands the application of teaching and learning standards as the drivers of learning-focused supervisory conversations. This work connects supervisory practices to current trends in education and to the skillful use of data, as well as illuminates the complexity of teacher expertise and the processes for developing it. Key ideas and central themes for each section are described below.

SECTION 1: Learning-Focused Supervision in Action

This section describes the four assumptions that guide the practice of learning-focused supervision. It frames the identity of a supervisor as a growth agent and offers a comparison of this approach with more compliance-oriented models. This section concludes with descriptions of the four qualities of learning-focused supervision that drive the skills and processes presented in the sections that follow.

SECTION 2: Four Stances: The Continuum of Learning-Focused Interaction

This section presents a Continuum of Learning-Focused Interaction with four stances for supervisors, arrayed from most to least directive. It provides methods for offering strategies and solutions while balancing that information with opportunities for processing and integrating. There are specific supervisor strategies for applying each stance, for navigating across stances, and for customizing learning-focused conversations based on a teacher's attitudes and aptitudes.

SECTION 3: Structured Conversations

This section introduces three templates for guiding teacher planning, reflecting, and problem-solving conversations that support ongoing learning. The templates incorporate current research on best practices for effective instructional planning, learning from experience through reflection, and increasing self-reliance in problem-solving.

SECTION 4: A Learning-Focused Tool Kit

This section describes and illustrates nonverbal and verbal communication tools for creating emotional safety and stimulating complex thinking. It provides strategies for distinguishing habit from choice when working with colleagues and offers tips and exercises for cultivating increasingly productive habits of practice.

SECTION 5: Data as a Tool for Growth

This section illuminates the importance of skillful data use as a vehicle for standards-driven supervisory practices. Essential skills include choosing low-inference data to avoid bias, increasing relevance, and reducing cognitive and emotional overload. There are also skills for applying data-driven feedback in learning-focused conversations using the Continuum of Learning-Focused Interaction.

SECTION 6: From Novice to Expert Teaching

This section describes expertise, specifically five spheres of teaching expertise. There are illustrations across a developmental continuum from novice to expert categorized by seven lenses for listening to teacher talk and determining effective entry points.

Downloadable Resources

This book provides links to downloadable resources, including a survey for assessing listening skills and a rubric for self-assessing supervisory skills. There are also tools for enhancing your learning and exercises to stretch supervisory skills using video. Look for the links and QR codes in related sections.

> "In any given moment we have two options: to step forward into growth or to step back into safety."
> – Abraham Maslow

The choices supervisors make and the actions they take shape the school cultures they create. Learning-focused supervisors organize and energize environments for experimentation and risk-taking in their schools. They know that when teachers thrive, students thrive. By pursuing their own learning goals, supervisors model the value for career-long professional growth. This book provides templates and tools for working more skillfully with a wide range of teachers to better support, sustain, and stretch their thinking and instructional effectiveness.

Notes · Insights · Applications

SECTION 1

Learning-Focused Supervision in Action

> **BEFORE YOU READ**
>
> 1. List some of your assumptions about the purposes of supervision. What are some ways your supervisory practices reflect these assumptions?
> 2. List three to five adjectives that define an effective supervisor. To what degree do these describe your supervisory practice?

Assumptions Informing Learning-Focused Supervision

In a learning-focused relationship, learning and continuous professional improvement are the hallmarks of effective supervisory practice. High-quality, data-driven feedback stimulates teachers' thinking about their work. To support the professional growth of teachers, learning-focused supervisors apply standards and structures for guiding their interactions with staff members. These patterns and practices initiate and sustain teacher learning driven by student learning needs. This approach is based on the following four assumptions.

Teaching is complex and contextual.

Teaching is a complex craft. All learners, especially the most vulnerable, need highly skilled teachers. Teacher effectiveness links directly to student success. Skillful teachers manage the social, emotional, and academic needs of increasingly diverse student populations. Total classroom awareness requires attention to all dimensions while simultaneously tracking the lesson plan, managing content accuracy, ensuring the use of examples, maintaining the clarity of explanations and directions, and varying the choice of language to match students' readiness and cultural backgrounds. Teachers provide relevant and meaningful tasks, attending to momentum and pacing while purposefully monitoring student understanding and adjusting as needed. This well-orchestrated approach organizes learning for individual students, small groups, and the full class.

Supervisor effectiveness links directly to teacher effectiveness. As teachers do, supervisors also work with an increasingly diverse population. In fact, the variation of teacher skill within schools is often greater than the variation among schools in districts, states, and provinces (Goldhaber, 2016). All this work is done in an ever-shifting context inside and outside the classroom. These dynamics include changing politics and policies, shifting societal expectations, breakthroughs in the science of teaching and learning, ever-expanding content knowledge, and new technological tools that increase access to information and support new kinds of learning.

Research-based standards define effective teaching.

A profession is defined by measurable product and performance standards. For example, doctors, lawyers, plumbers, and electricians have external measures that certify entry, define expertise, and establish the criteria for professional success. So do teachers. These public markers communicate that teachers hold themselves to high expectations externally in front of community members and internally among educators.

Learning-Focused Supervision

Well-articulated standards reflect the complexity of professional practice. Effective teaching can be measured and described by clear standards based on scales expressed in rubrics. These detailed descriptions provide common language and reference points for talking about teaching in a variety of professional domains. When supervisors and teachers operate with shared standards for what good teaching looks and sounds like, they establish common ground for meaningful explorations and purposeful goal setting. Thoughtful and thorough depictions of teacher actions and student behaviors establish the foundation for meaningful conversations about improvements in instructional practice. High-quality, standards-driven feedback establishes growth targets for all teachers across the range of teaching skills and experience.

Supervision is a growth-oriented process, not an event.

Learning-focused supervision is a growth-oriented developmental approach for supporting teacher learning that is part of the daily interactions between building leaders and teachers. In contrast with event-driven models that are exclusive to contractually mandated observation and feedback cycles, learning-focused supervision integrates with school life and can occur in brief hallway exchanges, informal classroom visits, and grade level and department meetings.

Like effective teachers, skillful supervisors differentiate their practice to increase expertise and support growth from novice to more expert career stages. Skillful supervision influences teacher commitment as well as both personal and collective efficacy. This growth orientation guides the choices supervisors make as they draw from a rich repertoire of strategies to meet both teachers' immediate and long-term needs. Effective instructional leadership matters for both teacher growth and student learning.
For supervisors, the ability to structure and facilitate learning-focused conversations lies at the heart of both one-on-one and collective work with teachers. Both skillful teaching and skillful supervision take years to master. There are always areas for growth. The primary goal of learning-focused supervision is to increase teachers' capacity to reflect on their own practice, self-assess, set goals, and monitor for continuous improvement.

The deepest purpose of supervision is to create a culture of learning.

A learning culture in schools makes knowledge public, spreads good ideas, and energizes best practices. A reflective and inquiry-driven environment increases a shared understanding of effective practice and provides a wide range of perspectives for examining critical issues. In these cultures, all teachers believe that they are held to the same high expectations for student success. Learning-focused supervisory interactions incorporate formative as well as summative data that provides essential feedback loops to guide planning and problem-solving and inform continuous improvement.

Supervisors need to believe in their own capacity and the capacity of others to grow. Learning-focused supervisors are a visible part of the learning culture. As lead learners and models, they set the direction for all adult learning. Such supervisors frame conversations by both what they talk about and the ways they engage others in those conversations.

Section 1: Learning-Focused Supervision in Action

Debunking the Myth of the Teaching Performance Plateau

One recurring tale in education lore is that teachers' performance plateaus as they master the basics of their craft. According to this narrative, teachers develop competencies to the point where they can efficiently get through the day and then slow down in terms of continuing to grow in their professional knowledge and skills.

A review of thirty studies published in the past fifteen years (Kini & Podolsky, 2016) debunks this conventional wisdom, finding that in many (but not all) cases, as teachers gain more experience they are generally and increasingly more effective.

Specifically, teachers improve at a greater rate if they work in a school environment that promotes movement off any plateau. Four conditions for success encourage this.

1. Effective hiring, induction, and mentoring processes and programs. This finding emphasizes the importance of systems for attracting and supporting people with a demonstrated passion for teaching.
2. Stability in teaching assignments. Like all forms of expertise, teaching expertise is narrow and based on grade-level and subject-specific skills, content knowledge, and cultural sensitivity to student learning needs.
3. Working in a supportive learning environment. This approach means participation in a collaborative culture, learning with and from peers in effective teams and departments, the presence of strong teacher leadership, and the use of coaching supports.
4. Well-implemented standards-based evaluation and supervision systems. These models provide teachers with detailed feedback about what and how to improve (Taylor & Tyler, 2012).

Embracing the Identity of a Learning-Focused Supervisor

Being a growth agent is the most important role of a learning-focused supervisor. Skillful supervisors understand that the purpose of their work is to increase teachers' individual and collective capacity for effective decision-making and problem-solving and to decrease their dependency on others to fix, solve, or rescue. Most importantly, supervisors do not see themselves as the fixer or rescuer. Supervisors who bolster a sense of efficacy in individuals, teams, and staffs promote the belief that personal and collective choices and actions can overcome obstacles to student learning.

In many cases, a growth orientation requires a shift in identity from decider/ manager/ fixer to problem framer/ goal-setter/ learner. Resourceful supervisors embody dispositions that motivate them to continuously hone their skills and build their knowledge base.

Dispositions

Learning-focused supervisors are inquisitive. They are more curious than judgmental and look for causality without impulsively taking action. For example, rather than praise or criticize performance when visiting classrooms, they consider and inquire about what might be motivating a particular action or instructional choice.

These supervisors are risk takers, willing to share their own learning gaps and goals. They model their own learning processes and publicly experiment, trying new things and asking for feedback.

Learning-Focused Supervision

For example, in staff meetings they might introduce a new protocol and invite colleagues to engage and then critique, or when collaboratively analyzing data, they might reveal their own lack of technical knowledge and defer to the expertise of other staff members.

In this way, they see and seek others as resources. They work to build resourcefulness in others as well. They believe in teachers' capacities for growth and presuppose positive intentions.

Learning-focused supervisors actively network with other building leaders, seek and nurture expertise within the staff, and support goal setting and goal achievement on a continuous basis. For example, such a supervisor might use a problem—such as a persistent learning gap—as a vehicle for bolstering staff skills in causal thinking, data analysis, and problem-solving.

Growth-promoting supervisors keep their eye on a vision for success while working incrementally to achieve it. They operate in the moment and over time, balancing a long-term perspective with immediate needs. For example, they support first-year teachers in core classroom management processes to build a foundation for deeper instructional work later on. Or if data reveal deficits in reading scores or if patterns related to fundamental skill gaps emerge, the supervisor engages with individual teachers and teams to design interventions to meet short-term goals and use them as building blocks for cumulative impact and success.

Skills

The dispositions that learning-focused supervisors bring to their work promote thoughtful attention to developing their own skills and motivate personal goal setting for increasing effectiveness. This pursuit requires commitment and attention to the challenge of breaking unproductive habits and establishing new ones. These skills, elaborated upon in later sections, are organized into three categories: structuring conversations, communication, and use of data.

Skills for Structuring Learning-Focused Conversations

In learning-focused conversations, structure maximizes productivity in a minimum amount of time. In these conversations, effective supervisors flexibly and fluently apply conversation templates to engage thinking and generate new learning. They are able to provide expertise while still offering choices and placing the responsibility for action on the teacher (see Section 3: Structured Conversations).

Skills for Communicating Effectively

How supervisors talk is as important as what they talk about. Skillful communication includes both verbal and nonverbal tools. Being present and fully focused on the teacher and listening without judgment creates and protects a safe space for thoughtful exploration of the teacher's practice. In this space, using language that invites thinking, clear pacing for thoughtfulness, and paraphrasing to align understanding all contribute to a productive learning-focused interaction (see Section 4: A Learning-Focused Tool Kit).

Skills for Observation, Data Collection, and Analysis

Facility with a wide array of data is critical for focusing effective learning-focused conversations. Fluency with multiple forms and types of data, both formal and informal and qualitative and quantitative, offers both a wide-angle and close-up view of the learning context.

While many supervisors are skillful with collecting and analyzing data, the difference for learning-focused supervisors is the way in which those data are shared and applied to teacher learning. When supervisors use multiple methods for collecting formative and summative data, eliminate personal bias and observe without judgment, organize and manage data sets to correlate with standards, and analyze data objectively to align with assessment rubrics, the standards and data become reference points for judgment rather than the supervisor's preferences (see Section 5: Data as a Tool for Growth).

Technical Knowledge

In a standards-driven system, supervisors need to cultivate a working knowledge base regarding teaching and learning standards, curriculum and instruction, formative and summative assessment, and both teacher and student development. Skillful supervisors identify what they know and don't yet know in any arenas and seek to fill their own information gaps (see Section 6: From Novice to Expert Teaching).

Four Qualities of Learning-Focused Supervision

Comparing Supervisory Approaches

As the various standards frameworks for teaching practice have been inserted into traditional clinical supervisory cycles, there has been little change in the intentions for supervisor/teacher conversations about practice. In contrast, learning-focused supervision is a reciprocal process in which ways to apply the knowledge base are personalized and constructed by the practitioner, not handed off by an expert or a program. In more conventional models, the supervisor identifies deficits, approves or disapproves of present practices, and offers fixes. In learning-focused supervision, determining the effectiveness of practice evolves through conversations that explore data and standards. As a result, the teacher takes responsibility for establishing and committing to growth goals.

Table 1.1 Comparing Supervisory Approaches

Key Elements	Compliance Models	Learning-Focused Supervision
Purpose/Intention	Quality control	Building capacity/growth
Intention	To fulfill contractual obligation	Knowledge construction
Use of Standards	Supervisor interprets and translates	Shared understanding and application
Use of Data	Prove/justify	Improve/illuminate
Source of Judgment	Supervisor	Co-constructed/shared
Goal Setting	Supervisor identifies goals to close gaps	Teacher identifies goals for growth
Use of Time	Calendar-driven events	Continuous process

Learning-Focused Supervision

Four Qualities

Four interacting qualities energize the process of learning-focused supervision. These growth-promoting resources are developmental, standards-driven, data-based, and customized.

Figure 1.1 Four Qualities of Learning-Focused Supervision

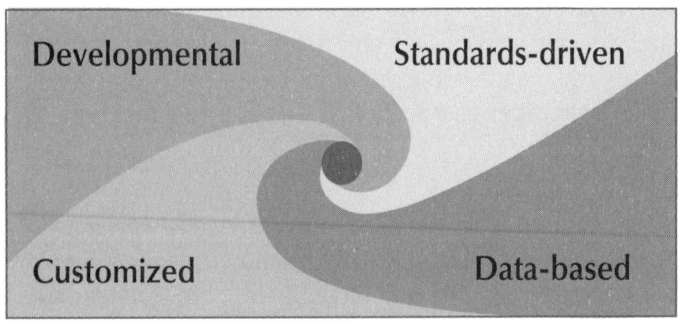

Developmental

Productive learning is always goal driven. Goals clarify the destinations for development. Learning-focused supervisors see improvement as a developmental process. Such supervisors view current performance levels as starting points rather than ceilings. They applaud progress to date rather than highlight gaps between present practice and expected standards. Performance gaps are seen as progress markers, not measures of failure. They see teachers as they might be and project positive images for success into interactions with staff members. In learning-focused conversations, teachers and supervisors identify the "not yet" aspects of practice, name next-level targets, and establish strategies to close gaps. Growth-oriented supervisors are goal driven and work with teachers to build the capacity to self-monitor, self-manage, and self-modify their practice for continuous improvement. A developmental approach strategically balances participation in this process matched with teacher readiness.

Table 1.2 Developmental Qualities

Supervisor Strategy	Definition	Action(s)	What it Might Look/Sound Like
Maintain a growth mindset	Seeing potential, not deficit	Clarifying success indicators when goal setting Presuming positive intentions	*"Given your goals for strengthening classroom discourse, what are some behaviors you hope to see and hear from your students as markers of progress?"*
Encourage self-direction	Building capacity to self-monitor, self-manage, and self-modify	Offering options Preserving choice Supporting self-assessment	*"Considering your lesson outcomes, three things that occur to me are…"* *"Given your vision for your class, which ideas might be the best fit?"*

Section 1: Learning-Focused Supervision in Action

Table 1.2 Developmental Qualities *(continued)*

Supervisor Strategy	Definition	Action(s)	What it Might Look/Sound Like
Balance nondirective with directive interaction	Navigating between coaching and consultation	Asking before telling	*"What are some ways you're thinking about more effectively structuring part of the day?"* *"In addition to those ideas, some other options you might consider are…"*
Mark progress at regular intervals	Noting benchmark achievement in both professional and student learning	Setting benchmarks during goal development Celebrating incremental success	*"So what will you look for at the end of the month to ensure that you're on target for goal achievement?"*

Standards-Driven

Frameworks that define teaching excellence and the related scales or rubrics for qualifying performance focus the standards-driven quality of learning-focused supervision. Standards frame shared expectations and establish and articulate measures of excellence for teacher and student performance. Illustrating specific standards in context—for example, what an environment of respect looks and sounds like in the first month of school or qualifying high levels of student engagement in a seventh-grade life-science lab—makes them concrete and accessible. Used effectively, they become rallying points for important conversations about instructional practice and the results of teaching choices. Standards not only structure expectations; they also raise them. By focusing on ideals, learning-focused interactions become conversations about desired results. Any gaps between present performance and those results are not about personal failings on the part of the teacher.

Table 1.3 Standards-Driven Qualities

Supervisor Strategy	Definition	Action(s)	What it Might Look/Sound Like
Consistently reference agreed-upon teaching and learning standards	Clearly articulated standards frame expectations	Standards documents are physically present during learning-focused conversations	*"Let's look at the standard for high levels of student engagement and generate examples for your class."*
Apply standards to assess performance	Clearly articulated standards establish measures of success	Standards, rubrics, and supporting data are used to document goal achievement	*"Referencing the video of your recent lesson and the rubric, how would you rate the quality of your questions?"*
Use standards to raise expectations for teacher and student growth	Clearly articulated standards with related rubrics illuminate directions for growth	Standards and rubrics are available to delineate growth goals	*"Now that transitions are smooth and time on task is improving, let's look at the teaching rubric to identify next-level goals."*

Learning-Focused Supervision

> ### The Battle of the Standard
> In English, the term "standard" first came into general use in 1138 after the Battle of the Standard, also known as the Battle of Northallerton. In this encounter, English forces repelled a Scottish army near a town in northern England. To help organize their forces, the English troops erected a ship's mast on a cart located on a small hill on the battlefield. Attached to the mast, each English nobleman had an identifying pennant—or standard—as a rallying point. In the swirl of battle, if a soldier was separated from his compatriots, he could head for the standard as a way to regroup and rejoin the fight. Embedded in the term is the notion of authority.

Data-Based

Data is at the center of learning-focused supervision, grounding conversations in concrete images of teacher and student behaviors and performance. Literal notes, student work products, and other forms of information focus the conversation on tangible evidence that becomes a catalyst for exploration and analysis. These data are the foundation for calibrating performance against clear standards, stimulating goal setting, and clarifying desirable and measurable results.

In learning-focused conversations, data serve to enhance understanding and perspective, create focus for monitoring progress, inform planning and decision-making, support problem-solving and goal setting, and generate new learning opportunities.

Table 1.4 Data-Based Qualities

Supervisor Strategy	Definition	Action(s)	What it Might Look/Sound Like
Create focus and monitor progress with low-inference data	Judgment is based on literal notes and multiple types of data, not opinion or preference	Collecting or gathering concrete data for use in learning-focused conversations	*"These data indicate a 15% gain in reading achievement for the targeted students. Combined with the reading logs you provided, it's clear that the new strategies you've incorporated are increasing success for these learners."*
Use data to support problem-solving and goal setting	Data are used to frame and define a problem and desired outcomes	Targeting relevant data for efficient problem exploration Using data for gap analysis	*"These data reveal significant differences in students' abilities to draw conclusions. What's your hunch about what might be causing those discrepancies?"*
Use data to enlarge perspectives	Data provide possible vantage points for viewing instructional issues	Collaboratively inquiring into the data to discover and analyze current practice	*"As we examine these data, let's look for indicators of improvement by standard and then consider some of the causes of those results."*

Customized

Productive supervisory practices are customized to match the learning needs of individual teachers for greatest impact. During planning, reflecting, and problem-solving conversations, skilled supervisors apply teaching and learning standards to the context of the practitioner. They illuminate and clarify expectations using examples based on the teaching assignment, grade level, or content area. They incorporate and consider time of year, years of teaching experience, and the implementation of any current initiatives. By attending to teachers as individuals, skillful supervisors personalize their adult-learning relationships to create safe environments for risk-taking. Flexibility with language, learning styles, and teaching models as well as facility with the full array of supervisory templates and tools described in this book provide essential resources for helping teachers stretch, grow, and see themselves as capable learners of the art and science of teaching.

Table 1.5 Customized Qualities

Supervisor Strategy	Definition	Action(s)	What it Might Look/Sound Like
Apply standards to individual teachers	Effective conversations are influenced by context: teacher's grade level, content area, teaching experience	Being familiar with the teacher's classroom, teaching style, values, level of content knowledge, etc. Having clear and relevant examples	*"Given your value for building collaborative skills early in the year, what are some ways you might adapt the strategies you used with your third graders now that you're teaching fifth grade?"*
Respond flexibly to teacher cues	Versatile use of tools, skills, templates	Adapting verbal and non-verbal tools to the teacher's communication style. Targeting elements of the conversation templates to promote teacher growth	*"You're describing a complex situation that seems to include three key categories: needs of struggling learners, the curriculum adaptations required to support them, and the instructional modifications necessary for their success."* *"We have about ten more minutes for this conversation. Let's focus on clarifying next steps."*
Pace to the emotional and cognitive needs and readiness of individuals	Considering time of year, level of experience, current challenges, and other factors, make choices that stimulate growth and don't overwhelm the teacher	Attending fully to assess current state(s). Monitoring one's internal voice and quality of listening. Balancing sharing information with inquiring about the teacher's thinking	*"At this time of year, the demands of teaching can feel overwhelming. What are some ways you can maintain the vision you had at the beginning of this semester?"*

Interaction Patterns Among Qualities

The four qualities work in concert to produce effective learning-focused relationships. While all teachers ultimately move towards professional expertise in all domains, the process towards growth is always developmental. A developmental approach requires customization of goals, strategies, data sources, and communication choices. That teachers are pursuing standards-driven goals is a given. Which goals and what data are used to support the process is part of the customization, and the scope and specific target area are developmentally determined. Similarly, which data are examined, which types and aspects of the data are brought to the table, and which data will define goal achievement are all aspects of a customized standards-driven, data-based, developmental process.

Implications & Applications: The Supervisor as Growth Agent

Implications

Learning-focused supervisors see themselves as growth agents who build teachers' capacities to make effective instructional decisions, learn from their practice, and become more self-reliant problem-solvers. Effective supervisors align their actions with that identity.

1. To what degree do your supervisory practices reflect the identity of a growth agent?
2. As a supervisor, what are some ways you stimulate teacher learning and growth?

Applications

1. Reflect on several of your supervisory relationships. Identify and list some factors that support your ability to develop and sustain teacher growth.
2. Given the factors you've identified, set several learning goals for yourself as a supervisor. Develop a plan for monitoring and achieving these goals.

SECTION 2

Four Stances: The Continuum of Learning-Focused Interaction

BEFORE YOU READ

1. Think of some times when you modified your supervisory approach with a teacher. What were some of the cues that indicated the need to shift from inquiry-driven to more directive approaches?

2. What are some ways you modify your supervisory approach when working with teachers across a range of skills and/or experience?

The four qualities of learning-focused supervision are present in every learning-focused conversation. In these conversations, accomplished supervisors apply a Continuum of Learning-Focused Interaction and shift among four stances—calibrating, consulting, collaborating, and coaching—to expand teachers' capacity to reflect upon data, generate ideas and options, and increase personal and professional awareness and skill. This continuum is an important tool for embedding two essential qualities, being developmental and customized, into supervisory practice. Adept supervisors specifically attend to being developmental and customized to support practice that serves the learning needs of teachers across a range of skill levels and experience.

Three attributes ultimately define the supervisory stance in any learning-focused conversation. One defining trait is the way that information emerges during an interaction. The second defining trait is the source of problem definition and gap analysis related to differences between planned goals and actual results or learning standards and student performance. The third defining trait is the source of goals for teacher growth.

In the calibrating stance, the supervisor performs these functions. In a collaborating stance, both parties identify gaps, gains, and goals. In a coaching stance, the teacher makes these determinations.

In standards-driven systems, supervisors purposely shape conversations. The ultimate aim of each of these stances and their cumulative effect is to support teachers' abilities to self-monitor, self-manage, and self-modify with increasing confidence and skill.

Figure 2.1 Continuum of Learning-Focused Interaction

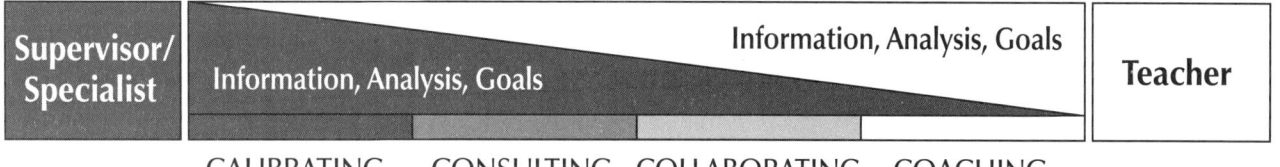

> "The ultimate aim of each of these stances and their cumulative effect is to support teachers' abilities to self-monitor, self-manage, and self-modify with increasing confidence and skill."

Three Supervisory Competencies: Fluency, Flexibility, and Fluidity

Developing expertise in applying the Continuum of Learning-Focused Interaction, like mastery of any skill set, evolves through three levels of competency: fluency, flexibility, and fluidity.

Fluency

The most fundamental skill level is fluency. Fluent supervisors recognize that they have choices in their approach to supervisory conversations. They are clear about the definition and purpose of each of the four stances and are able to operate across them with a repertoire of strategies for each. Verbal and nonverbal cues from the teacher inform both the choice of stance and when to shift stance.

Flexibility

With purposeful use, increased fluency allows for flexibility with the continuum. Flexible supervisors are able to customize a conversation. They understand that different individuals and different contexts require different approaches. These supervisors have internalized criteria for choosing a given stance in a given situation and are able to be responsive to a teacher's immediate cognitive and emotional needs while being mindful of the ultimate goal of development over time.

Fluidity

The third and most refined level of use is fluidity. Fluid supervisors are able to skillfully apply the continuum, seamlessly shifting stances as needed. They attend to both verbal and nonverbal cues from colleagues and listen and respond strategically. These supervisors have a level of automaticity that supports their ability to attend and respond to complexities and nuances, and they draw upon a wide repertoire of knowledge and skill to make a match that produces the most learning in the moment.

There is a sequence to the development of these competencies as they build upon one another. Fluent supervisors become flexible as they expand their skill set to include differentiated practice and the ability to monitor goals for teachers' development over time. As their integrated skill set becomes more sophisticated and nuanced, flexible supervisors can pay attention and construct responses with increased effectiveness and efficiency.

Being clear about intention as a growth agent and acting congruently creates a climate for thinking, risk-taking, and problem-solving. Attending to the relationship is critical to maintaining the emotional safety necessary for learning. When communicating, a teacher's outer cues, including intonation, gesture, facial expressions, posture, and muscle tension, reflect their inner processes. These indicators, as well as what the teacher says and how it is said, offer signals for determining an effective stance and fluidly applying the learning-focused tool kit. When supervisors embrace the intention to promote growth, they focus their full attention on signals from the teacher, draw on their repertoire of potential actions, and choose accordingly.

Section 2: Four Stances: The Continuum of Learning-Focused Interaction

CALIBRATE from the Greek *kalopous,* meaning wooden foot (in modern days this term describes a shoemaker's last). Taking this stance means that the supervisor determines and describes the fit between the teacher's practice and the expected standard of performance.	CONSULT from the Latin *consultare,* meaning to give or take counsel. This approach moves beyond simple advice giving. To offer counsel as a supervisor is to provide the what, why, and how of your thinking.	COLLABORATE from the Latin *collaborare,* meaning to work together. As a supervisor, this exchange means creating a space for true, shared idea generation and reflection with attention to one's own impulse control, so the teacher has room and an invitation to fully participate as an equal.	COACH from the French *coche,* the German *kutsche,* and the Hungarian *kocsi.* (Kocs is a Hungarian town where fine carriages were built.) A supervisor as a coach is a vehicle for transporting a valued colleague from one place to another. It is the teacher's journey. The supervisor is a guide and support system.

A Common Misconception

The four stances work in concert to balance information with the opportunity to process and apply it. A common misconception is a comparison between navigating the Continuum of Interaction and the Gradual Release of Responsibility (GRR) model of teaching. The GRR approach is an "I do it, we do it, you do it" (Fisher & Frey, 2007) and assumes the need for the teacher to provide the initial information and gradually, as learners gain more skill and knowledge, shift the percentage of input to more student-driven. This approach explicitly moves in one direction toward greater self-reliance, intervening with "I do it" or even "we do it" when something is not working. In contrast, while the goal of increasing self-reliance is similar, when supervisors apply the Continuum of Interaction, they flex as needed between stances in any direction. The continuum is a tool to balance responsibility for providing and constructing information.

The Four Stances

For learning-focused supervisors, the essential outcome is to increase teachers' efficacy for instructional decision-making and problem-solving. In this way, the skilled supervisor works to increase teachers' capacity for learning from their teaching while decreasing dependency on the supervisor to provide answers. In professional conversations, supervisors apply standards and communicate expectations as they support teachers in using data to determine performance gaps and establish goals for improving practice. Learning-focused supervisors operate across the Continuum of Learning-Focused Interaction to accomplish these responsibilities.

In each stance, the approach to these functions differs, as does the internal question supervisors consider when determining which stance to apply.

Calibrating

In the calibrating stance, the guiding question is "What are the gaps/growth areas indicated for this teacher based on present performance levels and the standards?"

The supervisor aligns data, teaching, and learning standards to a level of performance. Based on a variety of data sources, the supervisor determines a level of performance and organizes the data and the conversation to inform and discuss these assessments with the teacher. It is the part of the conversation when the supervisor presents the basis for judgment about the teacher's level of performance. This stance is essential when a teacher struggles to analyze their own practice based on expected standards. For example, a supervisor might provide data and highlight indicators of exemplary practice to motivate and clarify goals for a developing or proficient teacher. For high-performing teachers, calibrating is also the stance for illuminating effective practice that the teacher might not be aware of and/or motivating effective teachers to set increasingly ambitious learning goals for themselves and their students.

In some cases, the calibrating stance becomes dominant in the conversation, with a greater percentage of time spent there. Some triggers for this choice include teaching behaviors that create an unsafe or harmful environment physically or emotionally, inappropriate teacher responses, weak classroom management, student performance that is consistently below expectations, and ineffective instructional planning and delivery.

Functions

In the calibrating stance, the supervisor clarifies and reinforces teaching and learning standards and expectations. The verb "to calibrate" means an active process of matching an object or performance to an agreed-upon value. Simplistically, that value might be a shoe size or the diameter of a section of tubing. In contemporary educational discourse such values are expressed as standards. Important standards include creating a learning environment of respect and rapport; managing classroom procedures and student behaviors; communicating effectively with students, parents, and colleagues; engaging students in meaningful learning; and demonstrating flexibility and responsiveness based on assessment of student performance.

To operate with integrity within a calibrating stance, the conversation must be data-driven. These data are used to define gaps between expected standards and the present results and/or to reinforce and illuminate effective practices and establish professional learning goals. By clearly articulating standards, learning-focused supervisors define and illuminate problems. They present models and examples of standards in action that are content and grade-level specific and explicitly name expectations. In planning for action, skillful supervisors determine achievable goals, success criteria, and timelines for completion.

In most cases, the calibrating stance then leads to a rich conversation, which includes shifting among the other stances. This stance is the most directive of the four when used with low-performing teachers. Follow-up and follow-through on the part of the supervisor are vital to ensure standards are interpreted appropriately, performance targets are clear, and student progress occurs. Taking this stance is necessary when a standard or standards are not clear or when the teacher doesn't recognize the results of their own choices and actions. This lack of awareness can be true for both low- and high-performing teachers.

Section 2: Four Stances: The Continuum of Learning-Focused Interaction

Calibrating

Principal Robinson has conducted two informal walkthroughs and a classroom observation of Mr. Miller's fourth-grade class. The principal is concerned because in each case, two-thirds of Mr. Miller's students were out of their seats for much of the instructional period. Mr. Miller sits behind his desk and shouts at students to settle down. After fifteen minutes, when students do take their seats, only a handful follow directions and participate in the lesson. Mr. Miller's questions require only factual recall and are rapid-fire with no wait time.

Based on these classroom visits, Principal Robinson organizes her observation data and prepares for a learning-focused conversation. After greeting Mr. Miller, she refers to the teaching standards and begins: "Given the expectations for classroom management, at this point in the year students should be clear about behavioral expectations. Specific procedures need to be in place, and your students should understand the consequences for violating them. Transitions from one subject to the next should be smooth and take no longer than two minutes, with students in their seats with materials ready."

Referring to the time-coded script she created of the teacher's language and the students' actions, she continues by inquiring about the teacher's perceptions and interpretations. Mr. Miller is unsure of the connection between his behavior management, the data, and the standards.

Based on his responses, Principal Robinson says: "Given those standards and my observations of your classroom, there are two key areas that need to be addressed at this time. The first is managing classroom procedures and the second is questioning and discussion techniques. I've observed your classroom on three separate occasions, and these data indicate that students are inattentive and there seem to be no clear procedures or effective interventions."

Principal Robinson shifts to consultation and elaborates a menu of strategies for addressing these concerns, then asks Mr. Miller to choose one or several for his action plan.

"Another area for improvement relates to the standards for questioning and discussion techniques. Effective questions require learners to think and reflect, to deepen their understanding, to support their answers with evidence, and to test their ideas against those of their classmates. To construct thoughtful responses to these questions, students need at least three to five seconds of wait time. You'll see that the scripted data indicate only recall questions with one second or less for students to respond. You actually answered eight of the fourteen questions yourself. Further, there were no strategies for distributed student response such as signals, partners, or choral response."

(Again, the principal makes the data available to Mr. Miller.)

Principal Robinson refers to the data, drawing Mr. Miller's attention to the observation notes. "Right here, for example, you might have asked Rachel for elaboration. And here, students might have signaled agree or disagree."

The conversation continues as Principal Robinson names specific goals, identifies necessary next steps, and establishes a timeline for achievement.

Cautions

For each stance there are potential pitfalls. In the calibrating stance, it is easy for personal preferences to become prescriptions. It is critical then, that any judgments are data-based and standards-driven and supported by clear external criteria and evidence.

Avoid subjectivity or bias by using literal observation notes, specific classroom artifacts, and assessment data. A supervisor's inferences or interpretations can increase a teacher's potential perceptions of personal attack.

Learning-Focused Supervision

Table 2.1 Supervisor Strategies When Calibrating

Supervisor Strategy	Intention	What it Might Look/Sound Like
Share rationale for your starting point	Linking the teacher's and/or school or district goals to specific standards is an important criterion for your initial focus Sharing thinking reinforces the idea that the conversation is driven by goals rather than supervisor preference	"Given that your professional goal this year is…, this next observation will focus on…" "There are several standards-based areas to address in this conversation. I want to start with the data on student engagement, because it is a primary focus area for our school this year."
Use contextual examples to illustrate standards	Examples for levels of performance on specific standards related to the teacher's grade level, content area, or student population increases relevancy, clarity, and supervisor credibility	"The standard on student engagement includes choices and uses of instructional materials. Given your upcoming unit on immigration, materials that illuminate a variety of cultural viewpoints would likely increase both relevancy and interest for your students (autobiographies like… and nonfiction resources such as…)."
Apply a third point	Using a third point provides visual focus and increases psychological safety by separating data and information from the relationship	Examples of third points include: student work, observational data, standards and rubrics, video, etc.
Provide vivid data-based contrasts	Using data to contrast present practice with the standards-based expectation of performance (especially when there is a large discrepancy) captures attention and emphasizes the concern for addressing the gap	"Preserving instructional time is critical. When you're building in movement, the standard for effective transitions is two minutes. In this lesson, it took your kids six minutes to move from full group to small groups."
Illuminate the next level of performance	Clear performance targets motivate goal achievement Describing the next level of performance, rather than the highest, calibrates goals that stretch without overwhelming	"Presently your students are exerting minimal effort to complete the tasks you assign." "To meet the goal for students to increase self-motivation and take responsibility for completing tasks, you will need to focus on: • emphasizing the importance and relevance of the content, • clarifying standards and communicating high expectations while letting them know you believe in their ability to reach them, and • providing feedback related to their specific efforts and describing how they can continuously improve."

Section 2: Four Stances: The Continuum of Learning-Focused Interaction

Table 2.1 Supervisor Strategies When Calibrating *(continued)*

Supervisor Strategy	Intention	What it Might Look/Sound Like
Articulate next steps	Establishing concrete starting points with timelines stimulates action and builds momentum Timelines provide formative checkpoints for monitoring progress	"So based on this conversation, there should be rules for Chromebook use posted, modeled, and consistently applied by the end of next week. Then given that introduction, the next step is to develop and assign relevant starting tasks for your students. Finally, you'll need to create some simple assessments to be sure that all your students are using this technology as expected. I'll check in by the end of the month to see how it's going."
Offer feedback to amplify success	Highlighting success connected to progress toward or achievement of a goal builds efficacy and motivates continued or enhanced action This strategy reinforces cause/effect thinking and promotes transfer	"Eighteen of your twenty students raised a hand with comments and questions when you moved to different areas of the room to call on them. That is a significant increase compared to your last lesson when you stayed at the front. Given that, you should plan continued use of proximity to increase participation, especially when you anticipate or observe low student energy or engagement."

CALIBRATION VERSUS CALIBRATING

Calibration

- Is necessary in any standards-driven conversation
- Aligns performance to standards
- Can occur in the calibrating, collaborating, and coaching stances

Calibrating

- Who does the calibration defines the stance
- In the calibrating stance, the supervisor serves this function
- In the collaborating stance, the supervisor and teacher co-develop the calibration
- In the coaching stance, the teacher does the calibration

Consulting

In the consulting stance, the guiding question is, "What information, ideas, and technical resources will be most useful to this teacher at this time?"

Based on the teacher's responses to initial inquiries, the supervisor recognizes gaps in content knowledge, student knowledge, or instructional repertoire. In some cases, the teacher's problem frame is narrow or potentially inaccurate, or the range of strategies is limited. As a result, the supervisor shifts to the consulting stance.

Functions

From the consulting stance, the supervisor contextualizes standards by offering specific examples to ensure that the teacher understands expectations. The consulting supervisor offers perspectives on present concerns by naming possible causes and possible approaches to improve performance.

Beyond this gap analysis, a thoughtful supervisor also shares essential information about learning and learners as well as curriculum and content as they relate to existing issues, principles of practice, connections to expected performance standards, and relevant craft knowledge. By offering, "Here are some things to pay attention to," or "Here's why that matters," or "Here are some options," learning-focused supervisors make their thinking transparent. As teachers internalize principles of learning and teaching, these understandings become resources for generating their own approaches and solutions.

In planning for action, skillful supervisors propose a menu of teacher goals to promote student achievement and professional growth and provide opportunities for the teacher to choose and prioritize. Defining indicators of success and confirming timelines for completion are essential parts of the planning process.

Learning-Focused Supervision

Cautions

The verb "to consult" comes from the Latin *consultare,* meaning to give or take counsel. It is important to distinguish learning-focused consultation from simply fixing or telling. For many supervisors, the pressing needs they observe in classrooms trigger the impulse to help by providing information and offering advice. While in the short-term this inclination may reduce the burdens of busy teachers or temporarily resolve an urgent issue, context-rich learning opportunities may be missed if advice is the only resource offered. Further, advice without explanation of the underlying choice points and guiding principles rarely develops teachers' abilities to transfer learning to new settings or to generate novel solutions on their own.

If overused, the consulting stance builds dependency on the supervisor for problem-solving. Consultation that is learning focused within a professional relationship offers the teacher both immediate support and the resources for tackling future problems with increasing self-reliance, whatever that teacher's level of performance. Learning-focused supervisors do not allow their personal passion or organizational pressures to overcome patience with a teacher's developmental process.

Table 2.2 Supervisor Strategies When Consulting

Supervisor Strategy	Intention	What it Might Look/Sound Like
Offer a menu	A menu of options leaves the choice making and the responsibility for making a choice with the teacher If one idea is useful, several are even more effective Suggesting multiple possibilities when planning or problem-solving (at least three) provides information and support	*"Given your concerns about developing increasing participation, here are three options to consider..."* *"Given your goal to help your students think deeply about both content and learning processes, some ways to provide thinking might include: 1) pausing for 3 to 5 seconds after inquiring or offering a prompt; 2) using a think-pair-share protocol; 3) adding a writing step and have students think/write on their own before pairing and sharing."*
Think aloud	When a supervisor connects a specific strategy to the broader principles of best practice, the teacher learns to apply the principle as well as the individual idea When the thinking process that leads to a solution is made transparent, the teacher benefits from a deeper understanding of the process of problem-solving	*"When I observe students displaying behaviors like this, I first search for... Then I ask myself ... So in this case, you might look for..."* *"When I think about improving literacy skills for ELLs, first I ask myself what specific skills might be missing for these students, and then I search my current repertoire for effective strategies to meet their needs. So, in this case you might look for some formative assessment data to determine skill gaps and prepare some scaffolds and exercises to support development."*

Section 2: Four Stances: The Continuum of Learning-Focused Interaction

Table 2.2 Supervisor Strategies When Consulting *(continued)*

Supervisor Strategy	Intention	What it Might Look/Sound Like
Share what, why, and how	When sharing expertise, an effective verbal pattern is describing the what, why and how of an idea or suggestion This consulting move relates the what and how of possible actions to the purpose for these choices As teachers come to better understand these fundamentals, they are more able to generate their own ideas and strategies	*"Here is a strategy for addressing that issue (the what), which is likely to be effective because (the why), and this is how you might apply it (the how)."* (What) *"Given your concerns about behavior conflicts during small-group work, here is one strategy for addressing these issues."* (Why) *"Student engagement in the problem-solving process increases their ownership of both the problem and the solution. While this initially takes some time, it saves time in the long run."* (How) *"One way to do this is to have students individually write down what they think is causing friction with others and then name three possible solutions. Then have the students share these with one another and develop a shared definition of the problem and then select the most appropriate solutions."*
Refer to research	Referring to specific research-based best practices is often a productive consultation strategy because it removes any perception of opinion or preference This approach offers expert advice drawn from external sources that can be applied to the current situation For some teachers, this type of information adds credibility to a suggestion or idea	*"Based on your questions and concerns, the research related to these indicates that…"* *"The research on having students create graphic representations has been very consistent across grade levels and content areas. One application of those ideas to consider would be to teach your students how to develop cause and effect diagrams to illustrate important relationships in this history lesson."*
State a principle of practice	Connecting a specific strategy or solution to the broader principles of effective practice provides an opportunity to learn and apply the principle, as well as individual ideas, in other situations As teachers internalize the big ideas represented by principles of practice, they are increasingly able to generate or search for strategies that match these organizers	*"An important principle of practice related to [topic] is _____; so a strategy like [suggestion] should be effective in this situation."* *"Stating expectations clearly and reinforcing them through both repetition and highlighting examples of when students meet them is an important part of both managing student behavior and developing a supportive classroom learning environment. One way to do this is to create a chart stating goals, and during each lesson in the first weeks of school, ask students what indicators of success for meeting goals they see and hear."*

Learning-Focused Supervision

Table 2.2 Supervisor Strategies When Consulting *(continued)*

Generate categories	Ideas or solutions as categories provide a wider range of choice and a richer opportunity for learning than discrete strategies or applications A category such as "grouping students" is broader than "putting students in pairs" or suggesting a specific partnering strategy This approach is especially effective when several categories are offered for consideration	"Many classroom and instructional issues involve multiple categories of thinking and planning. In this case you need to consider… and… and…" "Broad categories of successful classroom management include attention moves, establishing routines, maintaining momentum, and developing effective transitions between activities. You might consider which of these would be the most effective starting point."
Name causal factors	Models the analytical habits of expert teachers who search for academic and behavioral sources that might produce any observable outcomes about which they have concerns Rather than suggesting potential solutions, it can be very productive to offer several factors that might produce a problem	"There are several things that typically would produce that behavior (or result). For example, _____, _____ or _____." "Given your goal of increasing student engagement, some factors that might be at play are: 1) they may not have or be able to access prior knowledge, both from experience or previous lessons, 2) there might be a need for more scaffolding to increase confidence and success, or 3) there might be a need for more checks for understanding, as they might not feel accountable for the learning."
Consider an alternative point of view	When a teacher is seeing things only one way, supervisors stimulate effective problem-solving by offering multiple perspectives Offering thoughts about how others—parents, students, colleagues, or administrators—might consider the issue	"You seem to be viewing this situation from the perspective of… Some other perspectives to consider are… and…" "It's possible that your students aren't perceiving the purposes of the new reward system in the ways you intended. It might be effective to consider their beliefs about motivational rewards."
Reframe the problem or issue	Related to considering alternative perspectives, reframing is changing the context or representation of a problem, including positive or useful aspects of the issue and alternative descriptions of the goal or approach to the problem Expert problem-solvers spend a greater amount of time defining a problem than they do strategizing solutions Novel approaches to defining a problem not only release new energy and ideas, but often lead to more effective solutions	"You appear to be framing this issue as one in which… Another way to think about it is…" "There are several ways to think about classroom climate and culture. Typically teachers search for simple rules and fair consequences to apply equally. Another approach is to work from the inside out and support students with developing self-management skills to be productive classroom citizens and contributing group members."

Section 2: Four Stances: The Continuum of Learning-Focused Interaction

Consulting

Ms. Brighton, a second-year teacher, has been reviewing the observation notes provided by her principal, Mr. Grayson, in anticipation of their reflecting conversation after he recently observed a seventh-grade math lesson.

The data indicate that a third of the student responses to the practice problems at the end of the lesson were incomplete or incorrect. Mr. Grayson begins from a coaching stance, citing the data and asking, "What's your sense of what was happening for the students who were not successful?" Ms. Brighton considers this and suggests that these students may have been inattentive or confused during her explanations of the necessary math concepts.

Continuing from a coaching stance, Mr. Grayson inquires about formative assessment, and realizes that Ms. Brighton has limited repertoire in terms of checking for students' understanding as a lesson progresses. As a result, there is little modification of instruction during her teaching. He decides to shift to a consulting stance.

"It is likely that your less-successful students were confused early on. Consistently monitoring for student engagement and comprehension ensures that students have a good grasp of the building blocks before moving on. This practice is key to their learning success. One way you might do this is to pause and ask students to explain a key point to a partner and then randomly select several pairs to report. This pattern of 'pause, partner, and survey' increases your confidence and theirs that the fundamentals are in place as you continue or, if they are not, allows you to modify instruction to address confusion before moving ahead. As we review plans for upcoming lessons, please think about and indicate some pause points for applying this pattern."

Ending the conversation from a coaching stance, Mr. Grayson asks Ms. Brighton to clarify her understanding and confirm next steps.

"Learning-focused supervisors do not allow their personal passion or organizational pressures to overcome patience with a teacher's developmental process."

Collaborating

In the collaborating stance the guiding question is, "What are some ways to balance my contributions with this teacher's experiences and current level of expertise?"

The collaborating stance creates a shared platform for the co-construction of knowledge. In this stance, both participants offer ideas, perspectives, analyses, and solutions. In many cases the learning-focused supervisor shifts to a collaborative stance to increase the teacher's confidence in their own ability to analyze data, frame problems, and develop strategies. Co-construction by the supervisor and the teacher scaffolds self-direction and develops greater ownership of instructional issues and potential actions.

In this stance, the supervisor provides support for idea generation balanced with respect for the teacher's ability to generate ideas and solutions. A rich, inquiry-driven collaboration creates permission for the supervisor to add ideas and perspectives without dominating the conversation.

Learning-Focused Supervision

Functions

From the collaborative stance, the supervisor and teacher jointly clarify standards to ensure shared understanding. Together they use data to analyze gaps and gains between expectations and current practice. In partnership, they analyze problems, generate potential causal theories, develop ideas, and produce strategies for action. Shared perspectives lead to greater insights for both teacher and supervisor.

Each stance is in large part defined by which participant in the conversation is producing the information and/or analysis at a given moment. The collaborative stance has the widest range of participation. In this stance, each party contributes; however, the supervisor might lean more towards consulting by suggesting criteria or offering a principle of practice upon which to base the ideas. Or the supervisor might lead with a completely open-ended inquiry which leans more towards coaching.

Collaborating

Mr. Ruiz always looks forward to a lively engagement with Mr. Mathers after observing his tenth-grade English class. Given the new curriculum, Mr. Mathers and his department colleagues are exploring strategies for increasing students' skills with assessing and revising their own written work. For this conversation, the principal and teacher each have a copy of the collected observational data as well as student writing samples to focus their reflection.

The unit objectives included students' ability to articulate a persuasive argument in writing, supported by text-based evidence. During his observation, Mr. Ruiz noted that students worked as peer editors with the writing rubric between them, comparing their completed work to the learning standard. Mr. Mathers started the lesson with a review of the rubric and directed the students to use it to assess their essays. He rotated among the working groups during class time. At the end of the period, he collected the edited work.

Mr. Ruiz begins the reflection from a coaching stance. Early in the conversation, he inquires about Mr. Mather's impressions of the collected student work. Mr. Mather's shares that the work was inconsistent and only a third of the students were able to clearly connect their own writing to a point on the rubric and use the standards to revise their work. As this was a new approach, he is not surprised by these results, but would like to figure out how to improve and is uncertain about what specifically might have caused the lack of success.

Shifting to a collaborative stance, Mr. Ruiz suggests that they generate some potential causal factors. Based on their shared analyses, the list includes poor choice of topic for this class, general gaps in written expression, lack of inferential reasoning skills, inability to incorporate text-based evidence, and a lack of clarity about the rubric.

Mr. Mathers considers this list and eliminates the skill-based causes based on his students' generally successful performance on previous written assignments. He determines that the most likely cause involves use of the rubric and peer editing as a learning approach, especially since both of these practices are new to him and his class.

As a result, Mr. Mathers proposes that his students could use more models of both the rubric and of strategies for peer editing. He decides to design a whole class lesson demonstrating editing and revision using the rubric. Mr. Ruiz chimes in with thoughts about guided practice using specific language that tenth graders might use so they feel confident correcting their peers.

Mr. Ruiz suggests, "Let's think about ways to monitor students' success. What will you look for to know that this approach is working?" They continue generating ideas. Concluding the conversation from a coaching stance, Mr. Ruiz asks, "What are some specific next steps you're taking away from this conversation?"

Section 2: Four Stances: The Continuum of Learning-Focused Interaction

Cautions

To collaborate with integrity, supervisors need to resist their own impulses to dominate and provide the bulk of the analysis and thinking. It is important to purposefully invite and create a space for teacher contributions. Pausing to allow teachers time to think and prompting and encouraging idea production communicates a belief in the teacher's personal and professional capacities.

Learning-focused supervisors need to be especially careful to monitor for balance in the collaborative stance. Personal enthusiasm and interest in a topic or a strong preference for a specific solution may override the intention to co-create ideas and actions. False collaboration then becomes disguised consultation or tacit calibration.

Table 2.3 Supervisor Strategies When Collaborating

Supervisor Strategy	Intention	What it Might Look/Sound Like
Participate in a brainstorming session	Mutual generation of information is the most fundamental collaborative action The nonjudgmental quality of brainstorming keeps the exchange reciprocal Generate possible reasons or causes for a particular circumstance or event, a variety of ideas or strategies, potential solutions to a presenting problem, or interventions that might be productive for an individual or group of students	*"So there are some students who seem to get distracted easily during class discussions. Let's brainstorm some reasons why that might be happening."* *"Let's look at each of the possible attention moves you're considering and generate a list of pros and cons for each."*
Engage in co-planning and/or co-teaching	Working together to create a lesson or a unit of study and extending that activity by teaching together are natural expressions of a collaborative relationship For learning-focused supervisors, this option often results in greater credibility as an instructional leader	*"Let's think about the key outcomes for this lesson and which kids might need some special attention. What's your sense of that?"* *"As we review the plan, let's identify who'll take the lead on which parts. Where would you like to start?"*
Design and conduct action research	Extending the supervisory relationship into a formal action research project deepens the learning potential and encourages a spirit of conscious curiosity about instructional practice This approach establishes a norm of experimentation in the school's learning culture	*"So in thinking about students' writing skills, you're curious about how to improve word choice in creative pieces. Let's explore a few current approaches for building vocabulary and written expression and design a systematic way to see which are most effective for your students."*
Explore case studies	Case studies provide a context for dialogue about practice The open-ended nature of most cases offers an opportunity to consider the complexities of teaching Exploring a case study from a collaborative stance can be an intriguing learning experience for both supervisor and teacher	*"We can explore a few case studies that offer issues similar to the one you're experiencing with the conflicts in your classroom. That will give us a focus for looking for causes, considering approaches, and choosing some next steps."*

Learning-Focused Supervision

Coaching

In the coaching stance the guiding question is, "What are some inquiries that would stimulate/stretch this teacher's thinking at this time?"

The coaching stance assumes that the teacher has the resources necessary to engage in data-centered reflection on practice and modify and manage personal learning. Operating from this stance, skilled supervisors inquire to elicit teacher thinking, drawing upon their experience and professional knowledge. Emerging from the work of Arthur Costa and Robert Garmston (2016), the coaching stance is synonymous with inquiry.

Functions

In the coaching stance, the supervisor references teaching and learning standards and a variety of data as the basis for the inquiry. In this stance, teachers calibrate their own teaching performance to the standards. The supervisor invites the teacher's thinking about each of these resources as they relate to current issues. In this stance, the teacher is the primary source of problem frames, gap analysis, potential solutions, and strategies. Through an inquiry process, the supervisor's role is to enhance teachers' capacities for planning, reflecting, problem solving, and decision-making. Given that the coaching stance is one of inquiry, there are always multiple appropriate responses, and the supervisor does not have a predetermined correct or preferred answer.

The value of questions is that they influence the teacher's underlying thought processes. By inquiring, pausing, and probing for details as data are explored, the supervisor supports both idea production and the exploration of the "whys" and "hows" of choices, possibilities, and connections. This nonjudgmental approach, applied over time, enlarges the frame, developing the teacher's ever-increasing capacity for expert thinking and practice. The ultimate aim of the coaching stance is to develop a teacher's internal resources for self-coaching, so that with time and practice an increasingly sophisticated inner voice guides professional self-talk. In planning for action, supervisor questions guide the teacher's exploration of goals, success criteria, and reasonable timelines for action.

Cautions

In a coaching stance, supervisors reduce potential frustration by posing developmentally appropriate questions. These questions should stretch, not strain, thinking. Questions that require more knowledge or experience than is presently available to the teacher can create anxiety and feelings of inadequacy. In such cases, it is more effective to offer information from a consultative stance and then shift to a coaching stance to explore that information.

Effective questions should invite teachers' thinking. The syntax and intonation of inquiries welcomes multiple possible responses and does not signal that there is a preferred or correct answer. Supervisors should take care that their own preferences don't influence their listening or direct their questions (see Section 4: A Learning-Focused Tool Kit).

Section 2: Four Stances: The Continuum of Learning-Focused Interaction

Table 2.4 Supervisor Strategies When Coaching

Supervisor Strategy	Intention	What it Might Look/Sound Like
Frame standards-driven inquiries	When standards are focal points for consistent exploration between supervisors and teachers, they become shared expectations and drive thinking during learning-focused conversations	"What are some things you've built into this lesson that will reinforce the math standards you're working on with your class?" "Related to your goals for increasing student engagement, what's your sense of how this lesson went?"
Craft data-based inquiries	Data are a powerful catalyst for focusing and monitoring teacher and student progress Data-based questions ground perceptions in specifics and encourage teachers to objectively observe and analyze their practice	"As you've reviewed your formative assessment data, what are some adjustments you're anticipating in this upcoming lesson?" "Given some of the results you're describing, what are some standards-based skills your students might need to work on more?"
Ask questions that reflect a growth-orientation	Developmentally appropriate inquiries acknowledge the teacher's current level of knowledge and skill and stretch their thinking beyond it	"Based on your experience with teaching this content, what are some goals you're setting for yourself and your students?" "How might you compare your current effectiveness with giving directions to when you began the year?"
Inquire for examples when response is vague	Precision in language reflects precision in thought When supervisors inquire for specifics, they support clarity of thinking and create shared understanding	"When you say 'appreciate modern poetry,' what might that look and sound like for this lesson?" "So you were pleased with the lesson. What were some specific examples of success that you recall?"
Inquire for connections and relationships	Questions that promote connection making, stimulate cause/effect thinking, support pattern recognition, and inform choice develop the habits of mind that are hallmarks of expert practice	"As you anticipate the next unit, what are some connections you're making between material choices and your students' cultural backgrounds?" "What's your sense of how the collaborative group work you've implemented is influencing student engagement?"
Use your questions to illuminate expert thinking	The self-talk of expert teachers is qualitatively different than that of less skillful practitioners Supervisory questions that emphasize and model expert thinking enhance the teacher's internal dialogue, which shapes perceptions, choices, and actions	"As you think about the conceptual understandings for the next unit, what skills and knowledge might need scaffolding for student success?" "You made several adjustments during your lesson. What were some of the cues that triggered those choices?"
Ask about the thinking related to the teacher's source of evidence, purposes, and criteria for choices and actions	Questions that require thoughtfulness rather than just description increase the learning focus of the conversation and communicate expectations that continuous improvement in practice requires deliberate attention to the reasoning patterns for teaching behaviors	"What are some intentions for the elements you're building into your behavior-management plan?" "Given your assessment of the student work products from this lesson, what are some specific next steps you intend to try?"

Learning-Focused Supervision

> ## Coaching
>
> With most of her staff, Dr. Salomon applies a coaching stance during post-observation conversations. This upcoming meeting regarding Ms. Mahoney's sixth-grade class should be no exception.
>
> After teaching eighth grade for many years, Ms. Mahoney has moved to sixth grade and is challenged by the different developmental issues for these younger students. One of her goals is to establish a culture for learning in which students are highly engaged and self-directed towards high standards of performance.
>
> Dr. Salomon is familiar with Ms. Mahoney's classroom, having visited several times during the first weeks of school. This conversation involves a formal observation of a social-studies lesson. She has sent ahead a copy of her observation notes along with some questions to think about. Ms. Mahoney, for her part, has recorded some of her own reflections about the lesson.
>
> Dr. Salomon begins with an analysis question. "The data indicate that there was as much, or even more, student-to-student interaction about the topic as there was between you and the class. How does that compare to what you anticipated?" Ms. Mahoney shares that these basic interaction patterns are becoming more established, but that she's also focused on the quality of student engagement. She draws the principal's attention to some of the student actions indicated in the data. She has already coded the observation notes for instances of peer support and praise and has noticed that of her twenty-eight students, twelve exhibit these behaviors consistently, while many students don't do them at all.
>
> Dr. Salomon invites Ms. Mahoney to explore some causal theories by asking, "What's your hunch about what might be producing the positive behaviors?" The conversation continues. Ms. Mahoney thoughtfully considers her practice as she responds to each inquiry. As a result, Dr. Salomon maintains a coaching stance throughout the conversation.
>
> To conclude, Ms. Mahoney generates several new goals, and shares specific action steps for accomplishing them.

Cueing Stance

Supervisors signal the stance they are taking nonverbally and through pronoun choice. These subtle cues, such as posture, gesture, voice tone, and word choice, are indicators of intention.

When calibrating and consulting, the supervisor uses these cues to shift the focus from the teacher to the information. Posture tends to be a bit more upright, and the supervisor's voice is less rhythmic and more credible with a narrower range of modulation than the coaching voice. In a calibrating stance, neutral or no pronouns prevail. For example, "the data," "these students," or "this work sample." In the consulting stance, the supervisor uses the pronouns "I," "me," or "my" as in, "Here's how I think about issues like that," or "It seems to me that," or "Given my experience with."

When collaborating, the intention is to create a shared focus on the information. Supervisor and teacher are physically side-by-side, intonation is collegial and approachably confident, and inclusive pronouns are used. For example, "Let's generate some ideas for," or "What might be some options for us to consider?"

When coaching, there is increased eye contact and closer proximity, leaning in, and more rhythmic speech patterns than in the other stances. The supervisor's voice tone is approachable and invites thinking. This posture and intonation create a psychologically safe space for thinking and reflecting. The predominant pronoun is "you," as in "So you're considering a variety

Section 2: Four Stances: The Continuum of Learning-Focused Interaction

Table 2.5 The Continuum of Learning-Focused Interaction

Supervisor/ Specialist	Information, Analysis, Goals		Information, Analysis, Goals		Teacher
	Calibrating	Consulting	Collaborating	Coaching	
Guiding question	Given teaching and learning standards and present performance, what do the data indicate as growth areas for this teacher?	What information, ideas, and technical resources might be the most useful for me to offer this teacher at this time?	What are some ways to balance my contributions with this teacher's knowledge and experience?	What inquiries might stimulate/ stretch this teacher's thinking at this time?	
Function	• Clarifying standards • Using data to highlight gaps/ gains between expected standards and present results • Identifying problems/ successes • Naming necessary outcomes	• Contextualizing standards • Using data to illustrate gaps and gains between standards and present results • Offering information, ideas, and technical resources	• Jointly contextualizing standards • Using data to collaboratively analyze gaps and gains between standards and present results • Co-generating information and ideas • Co-analyzing problems	• Referencing standards as a focal point for inquiries • Using data to inquire about gaps and gains between standards and present results • Stimulating teacher idea production • Supporting teacher problem framing • Inquiring to internalize habits of mind for effective planning, reflecting, and problem solving	
Role in planning for action	• Focusing teacher actions/goals • Defining success criteria • Establishing timelines	• Proposing teacher action/goals • Clarifying success criteria • Recommending timelines • Providing problem analysis	• Co-constructing teacher actions/ goals • Co-developing success criteria • Agreeing on timelines	• Exploring teacher actions/goals • Eliciting success criteria • Clarifying timelines	
Cues	• Credible voice • Using neutral language, as in *"The student's work..." "This example..." "This standard..."*	• Credible voice • Using neutral language or personal pronouns, as in *"I think that..." "It is important to..." "Here is one way to think about that"*	• Approachable voice • Collective pronouns, as in *"Let's think about..." "How might we..."*	• Approachable voice • Second person pronouns, as in *"What are some of your...?" "How might you...?"*	
Cautions	• Take care not to let personal preferences become prescriptions. Judgments must be supported by clear, external criteria/standards. • Use literal observation notes, classroom artifacts and assessment data to avoid subjectivity or bias.	• Monitor and manage the impulse to help or rescue. Stay learning-focused and don't let personal passion overcome patience with the developmental process. • Be aware that overuse of the consulting stance may build dependency on the supervisor for problem-solving.	• Resist the impulse to dominate the conversation and provide the bulk of the analysis and thinking. • Monitor for balance in idea production. Don't allow personal enthusiasm or preferences to override the intention to co-create ideas and options.	• Reduce potential frustration by posing developmentally appropriate questions. Questions should stretch, not strain thinking. • Be sure to construct inquiries that allow for multiple responses and do not signal that there is a preferred answer.	

27

Learning-Focused Supervision

of approaches to ensure your students achieve this learning objective," or "What are some comparisons you might make between these quantitative data and your classroom assessments?"

Navigating Strategically

The Continuum of Learning-Focused Interaction is a vehicle for adjusting the flow of information to meet the teacher's present developmental level. To accomplish this purpose, the attentive supervisor shifts stance to balance information with inquiry. As supervisors become increasingly fluid with navigating the continuum, they are able to monitor and adjust stance to meet the teacher's presenting perspectives.

In this learning-focused model, the calibrating stance is unique. In this stance, the supervisor names gaps between present practice and expected standards. This stance does not produce the learning; it names the growth targets for the teacher.

Consulting to Collaborating
vimeo.com/miravia/
consulting-to-collaborating

Consulting to Coaching
vimeo.com/miravia/
consulting-to-coaching

Adjusting Stance

Skilled supervisors listen and paraphrase to understand without judgment (see Section 4: A Learning-Focused Tool Kit, p. 65) and consider stance-based options for responding.

Table 2.6 Adjusting Stance

Coaching to Calibrating	"So you're not feeling completely confident about the lesson. Given that your goal is to improve your effectiveness with orchestrating classroom discourse, the expectation for proficiency is that the teacher-to-student talk ratio would be weighted towards a greater percentage of student talk. The observation transcript indicates that you were talking more than 70% of the time during the lesson."
Coaching to Consulting	"So you're confused about what's going on with those three students during group time. There are several things that typically cause sixth graders to act out in that way: ___, ___, ___."
Coaching to Collaborating	"So you're excited about using graphic organizers to develop thinking skills, but you're not sure about a starting point. Let's generate some options that might work for your next social studies unit."
Collaborating to Calibrating	"So we've been noting some gaps in students' reading skills compared to their writing skills, and you're unsure about which are most significant. A rich vocabulary is necessary for students to meet reading and writing standards, so that will be an important starting point. You'll need to design ongoing development and enrichment, especially for those kids who are not coming in to school with expressive language skills."
Collaborating to Consulting	"So we've generated some pros and cons for random or assigned collaborative groups. Because your class is just getting started with group work, I would suggest that you compose the groups you think will mesh best based on both academic and social skills and then observe how the groups work."
Collaborating to Coaching	"So we've generated several ideas for using learning centers. Given what you know about your students and some upcoming topics, where might you begin?"
Consulting to Calibrating	"Given this menu of options, you will need to begin with... because..."

Table 2.6 Adjusting Stance *(continued)*

Consulting to Collaborating	*"Given the possible causes I just listed, let's explore which is most likely in this situation."*
Consulting to Coaching	*"To ensure students can self-manage during lab, they need clear routines, assigned roles, and specific locations for materials and tools. As you consider your current classroom organization, might any of these need to be added or reinforced?"*
Calibrating to Consulting	*"The data indicate that there are patterns of low performance in content-area reading among children of color. Some ways to increase comprehension skills would be using culturally responsive materials, identifying and reinforcing key vocabulary for science and social studies units, and creating purposeful partnerships based on demographics and reading skills."*
Calibrating to Collaborating	*"Given the high level of parent involvement in your classroom, it's clear your outreach and ways of communicating are very effective. Let's generate some ways you can share your strategies and be a resource for your colleagues."*
Calibrating to Coaching	*"Given that these data show your increased use of both wait time and open-ended questions, what are some additional strategies you might incorporate to promote higher-level thinking in your classroom?"*

Six Supervisor Strategies When Navigating the Continuum of Learning-Focused Interaction

Six principles guide best practice in navigating the Continuum of Learning-Focused Interaction. These principles work in concert to maximize the potential of the learning-focused exchange, both in the moment and over time.

Table 2.7 Six Supervisor Strategies When Navigating the Continuum of Learning-Focused Interaction

Supervisor Strategy	Intention	What it Might Look/Sound Like
Start the conversation in a coaching stance	The response to an initial inquiry reveals the teacher's present perspectives, perceptions, and emotions The supervisor opens choice for the teacher, taps prior knowledge and experience, and acknowledges the presenting emotions	Open with choice: *"Given that there are data for two different standards, where would you like to begin?"* Build on experience: *"Based on your success with increasing student participation in third period, what are some ways you might incorporate similar strategies for your fifth-period class?"* Acknowledge the moment: *"What are some things on your mind that might provide a focus for this conversation?"*
End the conversation in a coaching stance	A final inquiry checks for understanding, agreement on goals, and clarity about next steps By responding to inquiries, the teacher forms generalizations and identifies specific applications	Generalizations: *"What are some big ideas that you're taking away from this conversation?"* Applications: *"Reflecting on insights you're forming from this conversation, what are some things you intend to try in the next week or two?"*

Learning-Focused Supervision

Table 2.7 Six Supervisor Strategies When Navigating the Continuum of Learning-Focused Interaction *(continued)*

Supervisor Strategy	Intention	What it Might Look/Sound Like
Embrace the blurry boundaries of the collaborating stance	The collaborative stance ranges from information (consulting) to inquiry (coaching) At the consulting edge, information becomes a stimulus for co-construction At the coaching edge, inquiry invites the teacher to lead while preserving space for the supervisor's input	*"Given the effectiveness of graphic organizers for ELLs, let's generate several that would work in your next social studies unit."* *"Let's generate some ideas for using graphic organizers with your ELLs. What comes to mind?"*
Use the consulting stance as a resource for stimulating thinking rather than for fixing the problem	To support thinking in the moment, supervisors strategically provide information, offer data analysis, and propose problem frames	*"One important principle of practice for emerging readers is to immerse them in a print-rich environment. A way to do that would be to bring in real-world materials like menus, cereal boxes, and recipes and incorporate them into your learning centers."* *"You believe parents are not involved because school isn't a priority for them. Another possibility is that coming into the school makes them anxious and uncomfortable."*
Shift stance to balance information with inquiry	Teachers transfer learning when they are able to take in information and apply it to their own settings Segmenting ideas with checks for understanding reduces the potential for information overload Offering information and then inquiring about applications encourages the transfer of ideas	*"Feedback to students needs to be brief and timely. One way to provide that is to move around the classroom to monitor students while they work and lean in to point out correct responses as well as those that need adjusting. Which of your students might particularly benefit from getting that type of input?"*
Apply the calibrating stance to judge the performance, not the person	Supervisors identify gaps and gains by offering feedback on performance rather than on the teacher's attitudes and aptitudes Objective data aligned to standards should be the drivers for judgment	*"These data indicate that 45% of your students have not yet met this writing standard. It is essential that all students master these fundamental skills."* *"Participation increased significantly in this lesson compared to previous observations. This change reflects significant improvement in communication with students and the positive quality of the learning environment."*

Section 2: Four Stances: The Continuum of Learning-Focused Interaction

Implications & Applications: Navigating the Continuum of Learning-Focused Interaction

Implications

Fluent and flexible use of the Continuum of Learning-Focused Interaction allows supervisors to customize their conversations by balancing information with the opportunity for teachers to process it.

1. What are some of your strengths and stretches in applying each stance on the continuum (see Figure 2.1 Continuum of Learning-Focused Interaction)?
2. How might skillful navigation of the continuum enhance your supervisory effectiveness?

Applications

1. Using the strategy tables for each stance, choose one or two new strategies to apply in upcoming supervisory conversations and then note the results of your choices.
2. Reflecting on your current practice, identify which stances you use the most. The least.

Focusing the Conversation: Establishing the Third Point

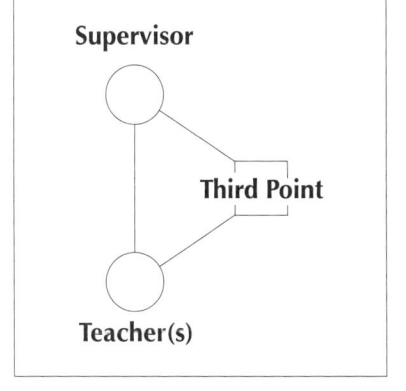

Skilled supervisors establish a clear focus for the conversation: a third point. As contrasted with two-point communication which is eye-to-eye and relationally focused, three-point communication shifts the cognitive and emotional energy from the supervisor/teacher relationship to the data. Effective use of a third point includes both verbal and nonverbal elements. Nonverbal elements include a physical shift from face-to-face to eyes on the data and a physical reference to the data source with a still hand, or frozen gesture. Verbal elements include using a tight, flat intonation or credible voice (see p. 75) and neutral pronouns when referring to data or information, for example: "the observations," "these results," or "this student work."

The third point is an observable focusing agent. In most cases, teaching or learning standards and associated performance rubrics are necessary third points for productive learning-focused conversations. Supervisor observational scripts, student work products, lesson plans, or videos are additional examples of relevant third points.

Applying the Third Point

Communications expert Michael Grinder (2006) describes the influence of three-point communication. To maximize the effectiveness of the third point, purposeful attention must be placed on the physical elements. The supervisor and teacher sit at a 90-degree angle so the supervisor can pivot from two-point to three-point communication. The supervisor's dominant side is toward the teacher so shifting to the third point closes the supervisor's body, directing attention towards the object. This relational exit assigns any emotion to the object, not the relationship.

Mediating Nonverbally

Physically referencing the third point in a space off to the side between the parties provides a psychologically safe place for information, concerns, and problems. This careful use of space and gesture depersonalizes ideas. It is now not the supervisor's information or problem, the teacher's information or problem, or even "our" information or problem. It is simply information or a problem about which and with which to think. Information placed as a third point frees the teacher to accept, modify, or reject the idea as an idea rather than as something connected to personalities. Thus, placement of the conversational focus creates a triangle, either literally or referentially, keeping the conversational container psychologically safe. Without this subtle, yet critical distancing, teachers may feel trapped by the relational dynamics of power and colleagueship.

Nonverbal tools, such as posture, gesture, and tone of voice, are all indicators about the stance the supervisor is taking. These cues reduce any potential friction, allowing for greater ease in the transitions between stances.

In a calibrating stance, physical and visual focus should be on the third-point documents. While referencing the documents with a frozen gesture, speak with a credible voice using neutral language such as "the standard," "this domain," or "the results" to articulate expectations and performance gaps. The intention is to make standards and performance metrics the authority and not set up a power struggle between supervisor and teacher.

In a consulting stance, the third point focuses the conversation on information and ideas and not on the supervisor or the teacher. In this stance, the supervisor uses a credible voice and at times it may be appropriate to use personal pronouns such as, "Here's how I've learned to think about issues like this," or "In my experience it often works best to." The liability is that some teachers, upon hearing the personal pronoun, will respond to a statement as a command and not a suggestion. When in doubt, use neutral language such as, "Best practices suggest that," or "Other teachers with this dilemma have had success with."

In a collaborating stance, supervisor and teacher are operating both physically and metaphorically side-by-side, dividing their attention between the third-point information and each other. The supervisor's tone of voice is collegial and approachably confident, using inclusive pronouns such as, "Let's think about this," "We might want to start by," or "Our next step might be to."

In a coaching stance, the third-point information is a catalyst for idea generation and problem-solving by the teacher. There tends to be greater eye contact between the teacher and supervisor, who uses a more rhythmic and approachable voice modulation to create a safe space for thought and reflection. The dominant pronoun is "you," as in "So you're noticing some patterns in your classroom routines that seem to be working," or "What are some ways you're thinking about increasing student engagement in your next math lesson?"

Because learning-focused supervision is standards-driven and data-based, the use of a third point is especially important in the calibrating and consulting stances. Physically referencing the third point depersonalizes the delivery of any information or judgment. It creates something to which

THIRD POINT EXAMPLES

- Observational data
- Samples of student work
- Rubrics
- Lesson plans
- Standards (content, student work, or effective teaching)
- Test results or other performance data

WHEN USING A THIRD POINT

- Sit at a 90 degree angle with dominant hand towards the teacher
- Eyes on the data/information
- Frozen gesture
- Neutral pronouns

NEUTRAL PRONOUNS

- "The data indicate..."
- "Given these behaviors, it is likely that these students..."
- "Based on these results, next steps need to be..."

Section 2: Four Stances: The Continuum of Learning-Focused Interaction

the teacher can attach emotional reactions. By purposefully establishing a third point, the supervisor transforms a potential confrontation into an opportunity to provide clear feedback. By reducing the perception of personal

---

Implications & Applications: Establishing the Third Point

Implications

Effective use of a third point in supervisory conversations provides focus, depersonalizes the information, and increases a teacher's emotional resourcefulness.

1. What are some topics with which a third point might make it psychologically safer for your teachers to engage?
2. What are some potential third points you might bring to your supervisory conversations?

Applications

1. Invite your teachers to bring third-point materials to your learning-focused conversations and share the purpose for doing so.
2. Practice the shift from two-point to three-point communication in low-threat situations. Focus on intonation patterns, keeping your eyes on the data/information, and using a frozen gesture.

---

attack, the feedback becomes information that can be heard and applied.

Customized Conversations

Skillful supervisors attend to the signals of the teachers with whom they are interacting to determine their choice of learning-focused stance. By attending to the teacher's verbal and nonverbal behaviors as they generate ideas and respond to inquiries, an aware supervisor can assess the effectiveness of a given stance and know whether to and when to shift stance.

It is apparent that not all teachers are alike. Customizing interactions to account for differences is an important skill set for supervisors. The supervisor's role is to continually increase capacity and decrease dependency, thereby empowering rather than enabling. Expertise navigating the Continuum of Learning-Focused Interaction is a key resource for matching supervisor moves to teacher readiness for learning.

The Intersection of Attitude and Aptitude

Teachers come with differing levels of self-reliance, confidence, enthusiasm, awareness, knowledge, and skill. These attributes vary in intensity and intersect with one another, resulting in differing degrees of receptivity to feedback, readiness to reflect, and resilience when confronting challenges. Experience is a variable but doesn't guarantee expertise. These attributes can also fluctuate contextually—for example, when there is a major curricular change, a new instructional initiative, a significant shift in demographics, or

---

"The supervisor's role is to continually increase capacity and decrease dependency, thereby empowering rather than enabling."

Learning-Focused Supervision

a grade-level reassignment.

We call these variables the intersection of attitude and aptitude (see Figure 2.2 The Intersection of Attitude and Aptitude). There are supervisor strategies for differentiating within each quadrant.

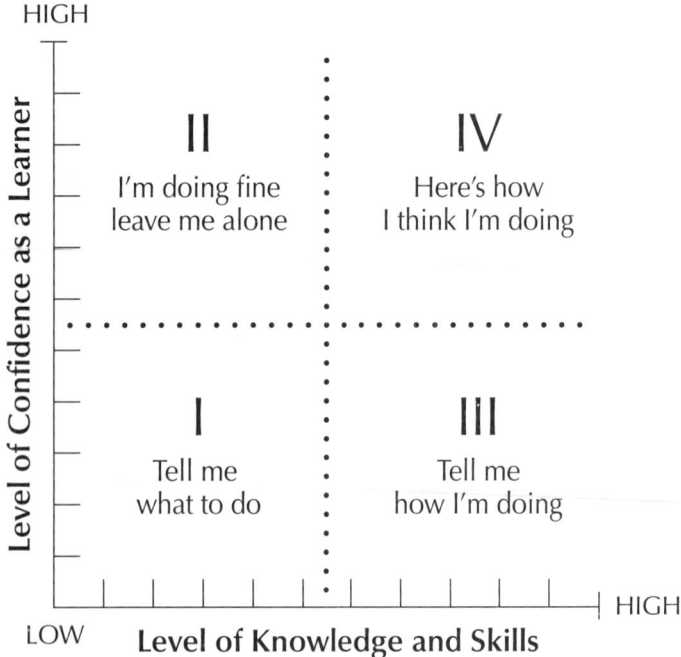

Figure 2.2 The Intersection of Attitude and Aptitude

Quadrant I: Dependency, "Tell me what to do."

A teacher in this quadrant lacks both confidence and skill. These teachers are easily overwhelmed by their teaching responsibilities. Their anxiety inhibits thinking and they become stumped when problem-solving. They are hesitant to act or try something new because they are fearful of making a mistake. Instead of relying on their own decision-making, they seek sure answers from supervisors. Rather than think for themselves, they want rescue and recipes. When working with Quadrant I teachers, the supervisor's goal is to scaffold choice-making and experimentation to increase confidence as a learner. In learning-focused conversations, there is likely to be a higher percentage of time in the consulting stance.

Table 2.8 Supervisor Strategies for Quadrant I Teachers

Supervisor Strategy	Intention	What it Might Look/Sound Like
Focus on consulting strategies such as What, Why, How	Consulting provides information to process, thereby increasing repertoire and the confidence to apply it The What, Why, How strategy connects specific actions with the reason for choosing them Making this explicit connection increases intentional choice-making and the ability to generate additional purposeful strategies	*"It is essential to provide expectations and criteria for success with the learning outcome and/or product for each lesson. This is important, because the clearer students are about what constitutes good work, the more they can self-assess and self-regulate. One effective way to do this is to display and review success criteria and rubrics related to a project or assignment."*
Begin by generating causal factors rather than offering solutions when problem-solving	Consult and collaborate to consider contributing factors and potential causes to increase expertise when problem-solving This approach increases flexibility and resourcefulness for the teacher as a problem-solver	*"Some things that typically produce that result include _____, _____, and _____. Let's think about which of those might be going on in your classroom."*
Emphasize the application of criteria for choice-making during the conversation	Consult and collaborate to generate criteria for choosing instructional strategies Applying criteria to options exercises the ability to make effective choices with increased confidence	*"So, you're establishing group work with your eighth graders. Some criteria to draw upon for balanced groups might include academic performance, social skills, and diversity (gender, race, ethnicity). Let's generate an observation checklist to use when monitoring group work. One thing to look for is balanced participation. What else?"*

Quadrant II: Complacency, "I'm doing fine. Leave me alone."

A teacher in this quadrant has more confidence than skill. These teachers often deflect the supervisor's overtures, claiming all is well. They talk with certainty and use the language of current initiatives and buzzwords without exhibiting the related teaching behaviors. Instead of seeking feedback and counsel from their supervisor, they assume they're going in the right direction. Rather than reflect on their own practices, they close their door and stumble forward. When working with Quadrant II teachers, the supervisor's goal is to increase awareness, to provide tools for monitoring effectiveness, and to motivate objective self-assessment. Therefore, in

Learning-Focused Supervision

learning-focused conversations, there is likely to be a higher percentage of time in the calibrating stance.

Table 2.9 Supervisor Strategies for Quadrant II Teachers

Supervisor Strategy	Intention	What it Might Look/Sound Like
Increase awareness by using low-inference, literal data and teaching/learning standards as a third point to calibrate present practice to expectations	Standards and evidence offered nonjudgmentally provide a foundation for learning Using a third point during communication takes the spotlight off the teacher, puts the attention on the data, and makes it safe to explore	"According to observational data from my last visit, 20 minutes into the lesson, 12 of 28 students were no longer focused on the whiteboard. How typical is that for this class?"
Inquire for details and specific examples Offer them if the teacher is unable to cite them	Asking first is always respectful and presumes capacity Specific details frame the conversation concretely Key examples open the territory for data-based analysis and planning	"What are some examples of cues you pay attention to when deciding whether to adjust or move on in your lesson?"
Visit the classroom regularly and engage in brief learning-focused exchanges	Nonthreatening presence in the classroom increases options for and openness to talking about teaching and learning This practice provides informal opportunities to gather formative data, explore success indicators, and promote reflection	"Before we end this meeting, let's agree on a few times next week when I might stop by and observe you trying out these new strategies. Then we can meet at the end of the week to talk about them."

Quadrant III: Uncertainty, "Tell me how I'm doing."

A teacher in this quadrant is competent not confident. They have fundamentally sound knowledge and skills but are insecure about their effectiveness. While these teachers make adjustments based on the demands of their role, they still seek external validation and rely on the supervisor's judgement, instead of on their own. Even teachers who have some years of experience stay in their comfort zone by sticking with what has worked rather than trying new ideas to expand their repertoire. When working with Quadrant III teachers, the supervisor's goal is to provide tools for monitoring practices, to support internalization of criteria for success, and

Section 2: Four Stances: The Continuum of Learning-Focused Interaction

to encourage self-assessment. In learning-focused conversations, the supervisor is likely to operate more of the time in the collaborating stance to balance emotional support with cognitive challenge.

Table 2.10 Supervisor Strategies for Quadrant III Teachers

Supervisor Strategy	Intention	What it Might Look/Sound Like
Co-generate success criteria and self-monitoring tools	The coaching edge of the collaborative stance balances supports with challenges and pushes thinking but does not overwhelm Creating success criteria fuels professional vision and supports the idea that the locus of control lives within the teacher	*"Let's think about ways to increase the collaborative skills students need to be successful with your science lab tasks. We can turn that into a checklist for formative assessment of student growth in that area."*
Extrapolate principles of practice by reflecting on success and generate additional strategies that exemplify each principle	The consulting edge of the collaborative stance is a resource for increasing awareness of patterns for success and generalizing principles of practice to transfer to future lessons	*"Clear directions with visual support and checking for understanding before proceeding preserves instructional time by reducing students' confusion about the task. Let's generate some additions to your present repertoire for monitoring understanding and choose one to use for an upcoming lesson."*
Develop an action research design based on the teacher's professional interest(s)	Self-confidence increases when teachers engage in safe experimentation When teachers explore practice systematically, the result is often increased efficacy, professional curiosity, and willingness to take risks	*"Given your curiosities about what motivates students to read, let's design some action research to help find out—maybe a student survey correlated to reading achievement data? Your research could lead to figuring out ways to encourage students who are less enthusiastic to read more."*

Quadrant IV: Reflectivity, "Here's how I think I'm doing."

A teacher in this quadrant has a strong internal locus of control. They recognize that their choices and actions are what produce results. These teachers have the confidence to try new things and are willing to learn from mistakes. They are reflective and self-disclosing about progress. They seek out and use data to set and pursue new goals, and they understand that teaching involves continuous learning. When working with Quadrant IV teachers, supervisors add value by stimulating idea generation, broadening problem frames, enhancing learning from data, and encouraging them to be resources for others. They expand teachers' lenses for observing the results of their practice, accessing their options, and making increasingly effective choices. In learning-focused conversations, a high percentage of the time will be in the coaching stance.

Table 2.11 Supervisor Strategies for Quadrant IV Teachers

Supervisor Strategy	Intention	What it Might Look/Sound Like
Ask questions that require thought rather than description	Description questions consume limited time and do not add value to the conversation Questions that explore for purpose, criteria, and data sources for choices or actions stimulate thought	*"What are some criteria you use when choosing instructional materials for this class?"* *"What are some overarching purposes for you when determining homework assignments?"*
Use teaching standards as a third point to widen the lenses for examining practice and setting new goals	Standards provide a fine-grained look at the complexities of teaching Using exemplars within and across standards allows the focus to go deeper within a given standard or wider to include connections to related standards	*"As you think about the standard for managing student behavior, what are some ways you've learned to anticipate and head off problems?"*
Explore and expand personal learning strategies	Inquiring about learning patterns and successes elevates the importance of teaching as a learning profession	*"As you anticipate teaching this course for the first time, what are some new things you're looking forward to trying and some previous learnings you intend to transfer?"*

Versatility Matters

Expert supervision requires a repertoire of knowledge and skills for engaging teachers in productive formal and informal conversations. These professional resources provide the foundation for operating along the Continuum of Learning-Focused Interaction. Having access to one's repertoire opens up possibilities for successful learning-focused experiences and offers options for consideration when a given approach is not working. Supervisors need access to what they know and don't know to help identify gaps in their repertoire and consciously expand their own capacities as growth agents.

In any given conversation, any one of the four stances may be appropriate. Reading the verbal and nonverbal cues of colleagues and responding accordingly allows flexibility along the continuum and supports learning and growth. This stance flexibility is the key to successful supervisory relationships. Given the goal to increase teachers' capacities for self-direction, this means continually offering opportunities to think, reflect, and

Section 2: Four Stances: The Continuum of Learning-Focused Interaction

Implications & Applications: Customized Conversations

Implications

The intention of learning-focused supervision is to promote continuous professional development for teachers at all levels of skill and experience. Resourceful supervisors are versatile in their use of the Continuum of Learning-Focused Interaction to support growth for all of their teachers.

1. Reflecting on the Intersection of Attitude and Aptitude, where would you place the teachers with whom you have the most growth-oriented working relationships?

2. Reflecting on the Intersection of Attitude and Aptitude, where would you place the teachers with whom you have the least growth-oriented working relationships?

3. Based on your responses to questions one and two, what are some patterns or connections you notice?

Applications

1. Choose a teacher with whom you have a growth-oriented relationship. Review the strategy tables for each quadrant and select developmental strategies to apply during upcoming conversations with that teacher.

2. Choose a teacher with whom you do not yet have a growth-oriented relationship. Review the strategy tables for each quadrant and select developmental strategies to apply during upcoming conversations with that teacher.

problem-solve within the flow of the real work of learning to teach. The ability to continually anticipate, monitor, and flex stance across the continuum is a vital component in developing and maintaining learning-focused supervisory relationships.

 Notes · Insights · Applications

SECTION 3

Structured Conversations

BEFORE YOU READ

1. Think of a time when you conducted a particularly effective supervisory conversation with a teacher. What were some of the attributes of that conversation? Describe specific, observable behaviors.

2. Think of a time when you conducted an unproductive supervisory conversation with a teacher. What were some of the attributes of that conversation? Describe specific, observable behaviors.

"Receiving feedback sits at the intersection of two needs—our drive to learn and our longing for acceptance."
– Douglas Stone & Sheila Heen

Applying shared and agreed-upon structures to supervisory conversations maximizes time and also serves to focus attention by providing a scaffold for supporting and challenging thinking within a specified context. For example, when a supervisor and teacher schedule planning, reflecting, or problem-solving conversations, a structure for guiding the interaction offers a topical focus and permission to keep the conversation moving. A structure designed for planning highlights the cognitive outcomes that support effective planning, such as predicting, envisioning, and forecasting. It also reinforces the importance of outcome-driven (not activity-driven) plans with clear success indicators. A structure designed for reflection amplifies the opportunity to learn from experience and to bring that learning forward into future practice. It also highlights the cognitive outcomes that support effective reflection, including recollection, cause/effect reasoning, and generalization. A structure designed for problem-solving decreases the urge to jump to solutions and emphasizes the importance of framing problems and exploring causality first.

Structured conversations provide an opportunity for the supervisor to gain insight into the ways in which teachers think about their practice. In a structured planning conversation, the supervisor comes to better understanding about the ways a teacher thinks about curriculum, instruction, and assessment for a particular group or groups of students at a particular time. Structured reflecting conversations reveal what a teacher notices (or doesn't) and how meaning is made from observations. Structured problem-solving provides support rather than caretaking, which appropriately places the responsibility for implementing a constructed solution with the teacher. Each template applied within each conversation is a key part in the growth process, and results in increasingly effective planning, reflecting, and problem-solving.

In learning-focused conversations, the goal is to offer feedback that increases the teacher's capacity for learning and self-modification and decreases their dependency on the supervisor for offering solutions and prescriptions. Instructional improvement is a feedback relationship between two systems. What the supervisor pays attention to and how the supervisor responds is one system. What the teacher pays attention to and how the teacher responds is the other system. In well-implemented, standards-driven systems, teachers and supervisors have common goals for student learning and a shared vision for the desired qualities of instructional practices. In these settings, both parties pay attention to the same things.

The conversation templates on the following pages are samples of efficient guides for purposeful interactions. They are based on fundamental and current theories of learning (see, for example, Marzano, Pickering & Pollack, 2001; Hattie, 2009; National Academies of Science, 2018) that suggest the importance of clear intentions within a learning-focused interaction. The general templates are based on the three phases in the Pathways Learning Model (Lipton & Wellman, 2000).

Learning-Focused Supervision

Each template has three phases. Each phase serves a specific purpose. The Activating and Engaging Phase establishes context and frames of reference. It activates prior knowledge and experience, surfacing the orientation and perception of a teacher regarding the topic at hand. It engages relationship, as well as mental and emotional awareness, and sets the scene for a thoughtful, learning-focused conversation. The Exploring and Discovering Phase provides an opportunity for examining the details of specific events, making inferences and analyzing experiences. Finally, the Organizing and Integrating Phase supports generalizing from these explorations, solidifying new learning, and making a commitment to action.

Each of the templates serves specific purposes. The Planning Template supports effective thinking about lesson and unit design. The Reflecting Template is designed to elicit thoughtful reflection, derive new understandings, and produce transfer from one experience to many. The Problem-Solving Template focuses on framing a problem before seeking solutions. Notice that these templates are designed to direct attention and focus on particular cognitive outcomes. For example, when planning, the supervisor's paraphrasing and inquiry should cause the planner to predict, envision, and describe. While reflecting, the skillful supervisor guides analysis, cause/effect reasoning, and synthesis. While problem-solving, the search for causal factors and hypothesizing are key processes. Each of these structures guides thinking and produces inferences, insights, and new connections.

Applying the Continuum of Learning-Focused Interaction and flexibly navigating across the four stances is an integral part of applying the conversation templates. The prototypes are inquiry-based, or framed from a coaching stance in these examples. However, learning-focused supervisors shift stances to support a teacher in producing the information and thinking processes within each phase of a template. For example, from a calibrating stance within a planning conversation, the approach might include naming specific lesson goals linked to standards drawn from the content area of that lesson and naming explicit success criteria. Within a consulting stance, the supervisor might then offer a menu of possible goals from which the teacher can choose, modify, or adapt. As a consultant, the supervisor might also offer some possible success indicators for goals. In a reflecting conversation, the supervisor could choose a calibrating stance to share data and take a collaborative stance to join the teacher in brainstorming a list of possible cause/effect connections between what occurred and the approaches and actions upon which the teacher is reflecting. And in a problem-solving conversation, the supervisor might inquire from a coaching stance about the

---

Feedback-Intervention Theory

The pioneering work of psychologists Avraham Kluger and Angelo DeNisi (1996), framed in their feedback-intervention theory, offers important insights into the governing principles of effective feedback.

1. Successful learners regulate their behavior by comparing the feedback they receive with goals and standards to identify meaningful performance gaps.
2. Since attention is limited, only feedback that illuminates these gaps affects behavior.
3. Feedback directed at the self-identity of the receiver (both praise and criticism) reduces the cognitive and emotional resources needed to improve performance.

teacher's perceptions of a problem and then engage collaboratively in considering desired outcomes for resolution, or take a consulting stance to offer potential causal factors.

> ### EXPERT MOVE
> Skilled supervisors establish a third point during structured conversations to increase focus, clarity, alignment, and psychological safety. Third-point materials might be selected by the teacher or the supervisor (see Section 2: Establishing The Third Point).

Planning Conversations

Structured planning conversations offer important learning opportunities for modeling and extending the fundamental intellectual habits of goal-driven thinking. Effective teachers set clear goals for their instruction, identify specific success indicators, and design formative and summative systems for monitoring achievement. They also envision the lesson and anticipate potential choice points, problems, and contingencies should the initial plan need adjustment. Attention to planning and understanding the ways in which experts think about plans is especially important to the development of novice and low-performing teachers. Applying the template can help internalize important planning questions teachers must consider to produce high achievement for all their students. These questions explore key components, such as learning outcomes, student learning needs, instructional design, and assessment, though not necessarily in a linear fashion. Astute supervisors listen for what's been clarified and what is still unclear and then determine the appropriate sequence of inquiry. Doing so with the support of a supervisor increases a teacher's confidence and capacity for effective, independent instructional planning.

Planning Conversations Video
vimeo.com/miravia/planning

In the Activating and Engaging Phase, establishing the context for a lesson or event allows the supervisor and teacher to "get in the room together," both the immediate space of moment-to-moment rapport and the conceptual space of the teacher's classroom. A primary function of this phase is to listen and establish a safe space for engaging thinking. The supervisor's intonation and nonverbal cues are especially important here. Experienced supervisors preserve time for more elaborative thinking later by moving through this first phase as efficiently as possible.

The second phase, Exploring and Discovering, is where the bulk of time is spent in a typical planning conversation. The four focus arenas are arranged in order of priority. These priorities are especially important to emphasize to novice and low-performing teachers, who tend to spend more time designing activities and approaches and less time clarifying goals and success indicators. Reducing activity-driven planning is an important goal for learning-focused supervisors. Teacher thinking is revealed when supervisors ask questions to elicit knowledge and application of essential planning and preparation components. It may be that a shift to a calibrating stance could clarify learning standards, or a shift to a consulting stance would benefit the teacher who has difficulty generating goals and success indicators.

The third phase, Organizing and Integrating, emerges from the general flow of the conversation. The two focus arenas in this phase offer options for

Figure 3.1 Learning-Focused Conversations: A Template for Planning

Learning-Focused Conversations: A Template for Planning

ACTIVATING AND ENGAGING

Establishing Context
- What are some things about your students' readiness (social skills, routines, self-management) that are influencing your lesson/unit design?
- What are some of the skills/knowledge students will need to bring to this lesson/unit to be successful?

Naming Presenting Issues
- What are some special areas/student needs you will need to address?
- What are some issues you anticipate might influence student learning?

EXPLORING AND DISCOVERING

Envisioning and Clarifying Goals and Outcomes
- As you think about what you know about your students, and the content, what are some key learning goals?
- What are some ways that these goals integrate with other content learning?
- What are some thinking/social skills students will need to apply?

Specifying Indicators of Success
- Given these goals, what are some things you expect to see/hear as students are achieving them?
- What are some formative assessments you're planning for monitoring student learning?
- What are some data sources you might use to determine student success?

Choosing Approaches, Strategies, and Resources
- What are some strategies you're planning that will both challenge students and support their success?
- What are some ways you'll ensure high engagement for all students?
- What are some resources or materials you/your students will need to support and extend student learning?

Determining Potential Choice Points and Concerns
- As you anticipate teaching the lesson/unit, what are some choice points that might arise?
- What are some options for supporting struggling students and enriching those who need greater challenge?
- Should there be a glitch in Plan A, what might be some options (Plan B)?

ORGANIZING AND INTEGRATING

Naming Personal Learning Opportunities
- What are some ways that this lesson/unit provides opportunities to pursue your own professional learning goals?
- As you anticipate teaching this lesson/unit, what are some opportunities for exercising new learning/skills?

Identifying Next Steps
- As a result of this conversation, what are some next steps?

Figure 3.2 Learning-Focused Conversations: A Template for Reflecting

Learning-Focused Conversations: A Template for Reflecting

ACTIVATING AND ENGAGING

Recalling
- As you reflect on this lesson/unit, what are some things that come to mind?

Surfacing Perspectives and Perceptions
- In this lesson/unit, what was particularly satisfying?
- In this lesson/unit, what were some things that concerned you?

EXPLORING AND DISCOVERING

Weighing Priorities
- Given your impressions/recollections, what might we focus on that will be most useful to you?
- What are some examples (e.g., student responses, work samples, interaction patterns, observational notes) that stand out for you?

Searching for Patterns
- As you reflect on this lesson/unit, what are some patterns of which you are aware (e.g., student responses, time on task, student engagement)?
- Given what occurred, how typical are these results?

Comparing and Contrasting
- Given the data, how similar or different is what you anticipated from what occurred (e.g., student responses, lesson pacing, student work products)?
- What are some comparisons you might make between your own effectiveness teaching this lesson as compared with previous practice (e.g., giving directions, responding to students, making adjustments)?

Analyzing Cause-Effect
- Given some of the results you're describing, what might be some factors that influenced what happened?
- What are some specific choices you made/actions you took that had the most positive effects?

ORGANIZING AND INTEGRATING

Making Generalizations
- What are some big ideas you're taking away from reflecting on this lesson/unit that will influence your future practice?
- Based on this experience, what are some new connections you're making (e.g., students, curriculum, instruction)?

Developing Applications
- As a result of new learning, what might be some adjustments you're considering for future lessons/units?
- As a result of this conversation, what are some specific next steps?

Figure 3.3 Learning-Focused Conversations: A Template for Problem-Solving

Learning-Focused Conversations: A Template for Problem-Solving

ACTIVATING AND ENGAGING

Describing Presenting Issues and Concerns
- What are some concerns you would like to discuss?
- If you were to give this issue a name, what might it be?

Investigating the Problem
- To what degree is this a stand-alone issue or part of a larger pattern?
- On a scale of 1-5, what is your level of concern about this issue?

EXPLORING AND DISCOVERING

Envisioning and Clarifying Outcomes
- Given what you know about this problem, what would you most want to have happen once it is resolved?
- In contrast with the way you're feeling right now, how would you like to feel once this problem is resolved?
- Given your thinking at this point, what might be some possible outcomes?

Generating Indicators of Success
- Given your outcomes, what are some things you expect to see/hear as they are achieved?
- Given these outcomes, what are some ways you might measure/monitor progress?
- What might be some initial indicators that you're moving in the right direction?

Identifying Causation, Strategies, and Resources
- What are some causal factors you think might need to be addressed to resolve the problem?
- What are some strategies for developing the knowledge, skills, and attitudes necessary for success?
- What are some resources or materials you might draw upon to support your plan?

Anticipating Choice Points and Concerns
- As you anticipate implementing your plan, what might be some points of concern?
- Given your concerns, what might be some options should those occur?

ORGANIZING AND INTEGRATING

Establishing Personal Learning Strategies
- Given what you know about your own learning patterns, what are some strategies you'll use to keep your plan on track?
- How might you capture your learning from this situation to apply to future problems?

Naming Next Steps
- As a result of this conversation, what are some of your next steps?
- What is the first thing you'll need to do to get started?

extending and solidifying awareness and clarifying next steps. Over time, skillful supervisors note potential stretch arenas for teachers and select focusing questions and/or consultation within these arenas accordingly. For example, a supervisor might shift to a consulting stance and offer a menu of potential next steps related to the plan.

In addition, lesson planning is an important opportunity for supervisors to support the development of a teacher's thinking capacities (Butt, 2008). By encouraging detailed planning that explores choice points and monitoring strategies, supervisors help develop the habits of mind of skilled practitioners. For example, by observing and participating in a teacher's planning, supervisors gain insight into the teacher's mental processes and can develop tailored strategies to support and extend thinking about instructional design.

By noting where in the planning process a teacher needs the most support, a skilled supervisor can decide when, whether, and how to move from coaching to consulting during any given conversation. Structured planning conversations offer a supervisor insight into how the teacher thinks about important aspects of teaching and learning, including understanding student needs, curriculum implementation, and content knowledge. The learning-focused supervisor listens during a planning conversation for how a teacher determines learning outcomes, designs cohesive instruction, and creates formative assessments. The exchange allows the supervisor to note patterns of thought for this teacher and to choose how to support and when and how to stretch this individual.

Specialized Planning: Goal-Setting Conversations

The Planning Conversation Template is a natural scaffold for setting professional learning goals. During the Activating and Engaging Phase, the teacher shares initial impressions about any data that informs goals. The supervisor and teacher then examine and analyze data for gaps and gains during the Exploring and Discovering Phase. As the conversation progresses, supervisor and teacher develop clear and measurable goals based on expected teaching and learning standards. Ultimately, in the Organizing and Integrating Phase, they agree upon next steps for action based on the newly developed professional goals.

During the Activating and Engaging Phase in a goal-setting conversation, it is important to take some time to clarify the roles, responsibilities, and options available for both supervisor and teacher. Defining the supervisor's role initiates a partnership, which can be shaped and negotiated to serve the learning needs of both members. Discussing the expectations of each partner reduces the possibility of disappointment or miscommunication down the road. Sharing information about the four stances on the Continuum of Learning-Focused Interaction makes it possible for a teacher to request a certain type of interaction, depending on needs.

Use the Exploring and Discovering Phase to establish clear goals for the supervisor-teacher relationship, as well. Further, when a teacher clearly articulates their own learning goals, the supervisor can focus energy and resources on supporting the teacher to achieve them. Both types of concrete and specific goal-setting are important to a learning-focused relationship. The Planning Template is an effective structure for guiding these initial goal-setting conversations.

Learning-Focused Supervision

During the Organizing and Integrating Phase, complete the goal-setting conversation by having the teacher summarize their understandings and name the next steps or when appropriate, creating a professional learning plan.

> **EXPERT MOVE**
>
> Skilled supervisors push for clarity of success indicators for products and desired performances when goal-setting with teachers. They focus on descriptions of what goal achievement might look and/or sound like.

Reflecting Conversations

Reflection is not an isolated thinking skill. It is the composite of multiple cognitive processes, including recollection, summarization, analysis, cause/effect thinking, and generalization. Data-based reflecting conversations consolidate and extend professional thinking. These data can be both quantitative and qualitative (see Section 5: Data as a Tool for Growth). They also support the internal dialogue and habits of mind of continual monitoring and self-assessing. Applying the Reflecting Conversation Template scaffolds this thinking. Reflecting conversations typically occur after lesson observations or at scheduled intervals in order to reflect upon patterns of teaching practice and student learning. Reflecting conversations are especially useful at transition points in the curriculum, when unit topics switch, or at significant points in the school year, such as the close of marking periods. The use of literal data, such as classroom observation scripts, rubric-based analysis, and student work products, grounds the conversation by providing concrete evidence of the outcome of planned actions.

Reflecting Conversation Video
vimeo.com/miravia/reflecting

Here again, the Activating and Engaging Phase matters greatly. The teacher's issues and concerns and/or perspectives and perceptions surface here. Depending on what emerges, the skilled supervisor will select a stance to explore the teacher's current awareness. For example, if the teacher notes some issues of concern but not others that the supervisor deems equally important, the supervisor as calibrator or consultant may add these to the list of topics to investigate during the Exploring and Discovering Phase.

Reflecting on data with the teacher after lessons have been taught, supervisors support the reexamination of earlier thinking and help teachers make connections as they analyze successes and review shortcomings.

During the Exploring and Discovering Phase, asking the teacher to weigh priorities is not only a respectful approach; it also provides a contextually sound assessment of the ways in which this teacher is developing as a professional. Experts notice more than novices. By noting what the teacher is noticing and what the teacher is concerned about, aware supervisors select an appropriate stance to help frame the content for reflection or add literal data related to what might be missing from the teacher's recollections. For example, if the teacher does not accurately recall the level of student participation, the supervisor might calibrate with data regarding how many and in what ways students engaged and inquire about how this lesson compares with previous classes. Identifying the factors that produce a given result is an essential element in learning from experience. Understanding

Section 3: Structured Conversations

why a particular result occurred allows for transfer of success or improvement of less-desired outcomes. This phase is a prime opportunity for developing teachers' causal reasoning skills.

> **EXPERT MOVE**
>
> Skilled supervisors spend the greatest percentage of time during reflecting conversations in the Exploring and Discovering Phase. This practice maximizes the learning from previous experiences rather than prematurely moving to planning for next steps.

During the Organizing and Integrating Phase, experienced supervisors widen the conversation from immediate issues to the bigger picture. The connection-making, generalizations, applications, and personal learnings that emerge at this phase increase the likelihood of the transfer of new awareness and insight. This is the true test of learning-focused conversations. Building habits of reflection and supporting transfer and applications of learning is a critical responsibility for supervisors.

Creating reflective, self-directed practitioners is an important aspect of the supervisor-teacher relationship. Formal structured opportunities to do so make a powerful contribution to developing this disposition. Note that the Reflecting Template is designed to elicit personal discoveries, as well as new learning about teaching practice.

Problem-Solving Conversations

Problem-Solving Conversation Video
vimeo.com/miravia/problemsolving

In the daily life of schools, there is certainly no shortage of problems to solve. Often when a problem arises, teachers shift responsibility and blame conditions—schedules, requirements—or other people—students, parents, administration, colleagues—anything but themselves. A primary function of problem-solving conversations is to develop effective and efficacious problem-solvers who are willing and able to take responsibility for creating success. Problem-finding and problem-clarification are central features of expert thinking. Framing a problem is as important as generating a solution. Learning-focused supervisors help teachers keep the long view in mind while responding to the issues and emotions of the present moment. Hallmarks of an expert problem-solver include the ability to envision desired outcomes and consider what might be producing a problem before moving to strategies or solutions. Skillful problem-solvers can also articulate clear indicators of success. When time is tight or emotions are fraught, it may seem efficient for the supervisor to offer solutions. However, moving too quickly with giving advice or even taking a consulting stance can build dependency and reduce the very capacities needed for increased self-reliance and expertise.

The Problem-Solving Template helps to structure the conversation and develop and support the thinking skills of effective problem-solving (see Figure 3.3 Learning-Focused Conversations: A Template for Problem-Solving). The teacher's perspective is the starting point for the conversation. In the Activating and Engaging Phase, the supervisor listens attentively, seeking to understand the teacher's concerns and how they view the issue. This perspective then informs the conversation.

Learning-Focused Supervision

During the Exploring and Discovering Phase, the conversation shifts from the immediacy of the issue to the desired outcomes. The goal paraphrase (see Paraphrase and Problem-Solving, p. 68) plays a critical role here. Offering a paraphrase that focuses on the anticipated resolution releases the emotional energy needed for a productive problem-solving conversation. Clarifying indicators of success brings solutions into focus. Most important in this phase is developing an operating theory for what might be causing a problem before moving to a solution. Establishing these three key pieces of information, clear outcomes, specific indicators of success, and a working theory of causation, creates the foundation for generating strategies and resources for solving the problem.

The Exploring and Discovering Phase proceeds very much like a planning conversation as goals and success indicators are especially important to clarify. In addition, agreeing on the possible cause of a problem is key here and necessary before moving on. This process provides a reality check for the depth of the problem and for the qualities of possible best outcomes. A consulting or collaborating stance can be an effective choice during this phase, to help identify choice points, generate options, and choose effective strategies.

EXPERT MOVE

> Skilled supervisors search for causality with their teachers before strategizing solutions. Without this understanding, time might be wasted generating solutions for ill-defined problems.

In the Organizing and Integrating Phase, the teacher identifies the necessary emotional and physical resources and particular actions necessary for success. This process includes generalizations about the teacher's own problem-solving approaches and commitments to specific next steps.

As with all structured conversations, the specific instance—in this case a problem—is a vehicle for learning. Thoughtful supervisors use problem-solving conversations for two purposes. One purpose is, of course, to solve the presenting problem. The second, and more important function, is to develop increased expertise and confidence for the teacher as a problem-solver.

Problem-solving conversations can be scheduled or may arise spontaneously in the hallway or faculty lounge. Particularly in informal exchanges, the skilled supervisor uses the Activating and Engaging Phase to move the problem-solving process forward without taking responsibility for solving the problem. Such supervisors listen carefully to understand the teacher's perspectives and perceptions about the issues, as well as to understand the specifics of the problem. By paraphrasing, inquiring, reframing issues, and offering alternative frameworks, the supervisor models the habits of expert problem-solvers who spend more time clarifying and defining the problem than do less-effective practitioners. This attention to the mental habits of effective problem-solving avoids the potential pitfall of jumping to solution thinking prematurely and spending time generating possible actions for unclear issues or concerns.

As a result of guided problem-solving, the teacher has increased readiness and the cognitive capacities for owning and dealing with issues as they arise, resulting in greater confidence and effectiveness as a problem-solver.

Navigating Within and Across the Conversation Templates

We offer the metaphor of a map for the Conversation Templates. A map defines boundaries, clarifying what belongs inside and what is external to the territory. Likewise, these template structures provide clarity about the parameters of conversation. When used skillfully, they are especially time efficient, allowing either colleague to return to the agreed upon purpose(s) of the meeting. A map can also be shared so both parties know what territory can be explored and what routes are possible—whether to take the same path each time or vary it. Further, while each area on a map is clearly defined, the user may choose to apportion time visiting several neighborhoods or spend most of it concentrated in one or two. In fact, once the supervisor and teacher have had some experience with the Conversation Templates, they are rarely applied linearly. That is, moving from one arena (establishing goals and outcomes) to another (potential choice points) and then to a third (indicators of success) and back to the first (for more goals and outcomes) is quite common. It frequently makes sense to navigate across the templates. In this case, the supervisor and teacher reflect on past experiences during a planning conversation, finish a reflecting conversation with questions for applying new learning to a future plan, or begin a problem-solving conversation as a result of analyzing results during reflection.

It is important, however, to maintain the integrity of each template and be intentional if and when navigating to another structure. For example, it is important to take the time to go deep into reflection without the conversation moving too quickly to planning for next steps.

Integrating the Conversation Templates and the Continuum of Learning-Focused Interaction

Each learning-focused conversation is an opportunity to develop a teacher's thinking about their practice. Skillful supervisors customize their inquiries, collaborative suggestions, and consultative ideas during conversations by navigating the Continuum of Learning-Focused Interaction.

For example, in a Planning Conversation:

Starting the conversation from a coaching stance.

A teacher might say:
"I'm rethinking my geography unit about what makes a country a country. When I've taught it in the past, not all the kids get the big ideas."

A supervisor might respond:
"So given your experiences with this unit, you want to redesign it to ensure students meet the standards."

"What are some examples of the student misunderstandings that are of most concern to you?"

Shifting from a consulting stance to a collaborating stance.

A teacher might say:
"Some students seem to think that maps are settled features—that someone

Learning-Focused Supervision

just recorded what is fact. Many also think that borders and boundaries are permanent."

A supervisor might respond:
After a paraphrase: "It seems to me that when kids struggle to grasp a concept, it may be that they can't relate it to their own experiences. It might be a good idea to think like a seventh grader and discover what they already know about the geography, history, and politics of something closer to home, such as the U.S. or Canada, to clarify basic concepts. Let's explore some ways to do that."

Continuing in a collaborative stance.

A teacher might say:
"Well given the standard for being able to interpret geopolitical maps, kids need to know that there are natural borders and politically determined borders and be able to recognize and distinguish between them."

A supervisor might respond:
After a paraphrase: "Let's brainstorm some examples that your students might be familiar with, for example Niagara Falls as a natural border between the US and Canada. What are some others?"

Shifting from a consulting stance to a coaching stance.

After brainstorming several examples, a teacher might say:
"I think I can have students create sort cards with examples of different types of borders and work with them in groups. Then I can have them move on to large maps so they can identify a variety of borders."

A supervisor might respond:
"Given their present level of readiness, it might be a good idea to put students into pairs to increase focus and participation."

"As they work, what are some things you'll pay attention to so you're confident they're getting it?"

Ending the conversation in a coaching stance.

A teacher generates a number of success indicators...

A supervisor might respond:
"So as you think about your upcoming lessons, what are some next steps for you?"

For example, in a Reflecting Conversation

Starting the conversation from a coaching stance.

A teacher might say:
"I think I'm on the right track. The kids are making progress with this unit."

A supervisor might respond:
"You seem pleased with how things are going."

"What are some examples that stand out for you?"

Continuing in a coaching stance.

A teacher might say:
"I passed out copies of two different North American maps, like we discussed, one showing political boundaries and one showing geophysical features. I had pairs compare the two maps and note the things they saw."

A supervisor might respond:
"So you wanted them to identify the key features expected in the standards."

"What percentage of your kids were able to do that?"

Shifting to a consulting stance.

A teacher might say:
"I think most of the pairs noticed that some borders were straight lines and some were curvy lines. In each class, someone pointed out that the curvy lines were rivers when they compared the two maps. But I'm not sure how to get them beyond this point."

A supervisor might respond:
"So by isolating the central concepts, you've got a starting point for your unit and you're ready for next steps."

"In moving forward, the research on using graphic organizers to help students' conceptual development is very consistent across grade levels and content areas. In this case, you might teach them how to create spider diagrams to illustrate the various features that make a country a country."

Shifting from a consulting stance to a coaching stance.

A supervisor might respond:
"What are some of your experiences with using graphic organizers or this one specifically?"

Ending the conversation in a coaching stance.

After brainstorming several examples, a teacher might say:
"I've used them in other units, but I hadn't thought about it for this one."

A supervisor might respond:
"So you're thinking that graphic organizers might be useful in a variety of lessons."

"In addition to that, what are some other things you're learning about developing students' understanding of essential concepts?"

Learning-Focused Conversations: The Importance of Structure

We propose the conversation templates be used as frameworks and not like recipes to be followed in a step-by-step fashion. The questions within each phase beneath each focus arena are intended as models and possibilities, not as the only options. Different conversations take on different flavors. Although these templates are relatively generic, thoughtful attention to their use for specialized functions and in different contexts produces powerful results.

Each conversation template offers a structure to supervisor-teacher conversations. These guides enhance the efficiency of meeting time by providing a shared focus. They also serve as learning scaffolds, encouraging teachers to internalize the thinking protocols that guide effective planning, reflection, and problem-solving about their own practice. The questions and ways of thinking that are explored during structured conversations develop the cognitive capacities for expert practice and become an internal voice for self-directed growth.

As a result, after several cycles of planning, observation, and reflection using the conversation templates, the teacher comes to a planning, reflecting, or problem-solving meeting prepared to respond to the stimulating questions of the supervisor. This readiness and confidence sets the stage for increasingly rigorous conversations about teaching practice and increasingly effective solutions to the inevitable challenges of classroom life.

Implications & Applications: Structured Conversations

Implications

Effective supervisors apply structured templates to their learning-focused conversations to maximize focus and use time efficiently. Each structured conversation is an opportunity for learning that transfers beyond the specific event being explored.

1. How might increased skill in applying the conversation templates improve the effectiveness of your supervisory work?
2. Which conversation templates might be most important for you to internalize first?

Applications

1. During your upcoming supervisory conversations, use a printed version of the conversation template to guide the interaction. Note the effects for you and your teacher.
2. Share the templates and your intentions in applying them with your teachers so they can prepare for upcoming structured conversations.
3. To maximize your efficiency, flexibility, and focus during conversations, commit the template structures to memory.

SECTION 4: A Learning-Focused Tool Kit

BEFORE YOU READ

1. Given the importance of offering your full attention in a supervisory conversation, what are some things that might get in the way of being able to do so?

2. What are some of your nonverbal and verbal actions that create conditions for receptivity and learning? What are some that might do the opposite?

How supervisors listen and talk to teachers influences how those teachers learn from their work. In learning-focused conversations, supervisors and teachers listen and speak in equal measure so each party can be heard and can influence the thinking of the other. However, what supervisors say is not always what teachers hear. Effective supervisory conversations create awareness and shared understanding. To engage in such conversations, skilled supervisors make use of a learning-focused tool kit that includes both nonverbal and verbal tools (see Figure 4.1 Learning-Focused Tool Kit).

Like any collection of tools, these can be used with differing degrees of skill, need regular sharpening, and contain specialty items for specific purposes. These purposes include building productive working relationships, supporting continuous learning, and encouraging commitment to action. By listening carefully to teachers, growth-promoting supervisors tailor their responses to increase receptivity and stimulate thinking.

Figure 4.1 Learning-Focused Tool Kit

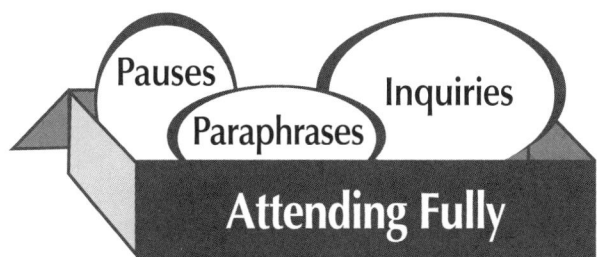

Attending fully is the foundation for the non-verbal and verbal skills that comprise the learning-focused tool kit.

The learning-focused tool kit presented in this chapter includes attending fully (physical alignment and listening), pausing, paraphrasing, and inquiring. This tool kit operates in concert with the Continuum of Learning-Focused Interaction (see Establishing The Third Point, p. 31) and focuses on the templates for planning, reflecting, and problem-solving (see Section 3: Structured Conversations). Being fully present is fundamental for applying these tools.

> "In learning-focused conversations, supervisors and teachers listen and speak in equal measure so each party can be heard and can influence the thinking of the other."

Learning-Focused Supervision

Table 4.1 Supervisor Strategies with the Learning-Focused Tool Kit

Supervisor Strategy	Intention	What it might look/sound like
Trust the power of the pause	Pausing creates the space for thought for both supervisor and teacher Effective pauses are tailored to match the cognitive demand and communication style of the teacher	During a learning-focused conversation, there are consistent intervals when no one speaks, both parties are focused, and signs of thinking are apparent.
Apply a pattern of pause, paraphrase, inquire	This pattern of discourse paces the conversation for thinking Pause allows time to think, paraphrase shapes the conversation and provides the emotional readiness to think, and inquiry pushes thinking past what is already known	Teacher: *"I've taught this unit for years, and I'd like to get the kids to engage more deeply with the content."* Supervisor: **Pause**, then **paraphrase**: *"So you have important content that you want kids to get more out of."* Then **inquire**: *"What elements of this unit might have the most potential for getting kids more involved?"*
Paraphrase as first response	Listening and then paraphrasing signals full attention and understanding (or desire to understand) and invites the teacher's confirmation or correction Provides a sense of where to inquire or what information to offer	Teacher: *"I have some students in my class who are ready to go as learners and others who hold us back."* Supervisor: *"You're finding that there are diverse readiness levels, and you want to be able to meet the needs of all your learners."*
Paraphrase before shifting stance on the continuum	The paraphrase affirms current understanding and signals the intention to "take the teacher along" when shifting stance rather than pulling, pushing, or imposing the supervisor's way of thinking	Teacher: *"I know the internet offers rich resources, but my students don't have good criteria for whether a site is reliable or not."* Supervisor: *"So you're thinking about ways to help students internalize standards they can apply to determine the quality of information they find online. Let's generate some possible ideas for addressing that."*
Construct questions for high thought/ low threat	Thinking out loud when you are uncertain requires risk-taking Designing inquiries using the elements of the invitation preserves emotional safety, invites thinking, and reduces risk	Teacher: *"My students don't stop to think carefully before they blurt out the first thing that comes to mind."* Supervisor: *"Given all you know about your students, what's your sense about what might be going on for them?"*
Ask more than tell	When inquiry drives the conversation, there is more opportunity for the teacher to talk and make meaning Attending to the talk ratio and information flow allows the teacher to influence the direction of the conversation	Teacher: *"I'm really stuck when it comes to developing more time efficient routines for getting kids ready to leave at the end of the day."* Supervisor: *"Students need predictable procedures that they can perform automatically. What are some of the desired actions you want them to take?"*

Section 4: A Learning-Focused Tool Kit

The Habit Cycle

All communication patterns are built on a set of personal habits. We acquire habits from our families, native cultures, and home regions. Learning new communication behaviors requires recognizing and unlearning old routines and developing new ones. The Habit Cycle explains how this process influences our behaviors and offers ways to develop more productive supervisory communications skills.

"Habit is the intersection of knowledge (what to do), skill (how to do), and desire (want to do)."
– Stephen Covey

Skilled supervisors distinguish between habit and choice. Habits are neurological patterns that are reinforced by repetition. Charles Duhigg (2012) describes a habit cycle that includes a cue, an embedded routine, and some form of reward. Habits are mentally and emotionally efficient and are developed over years of practice. Communication patterns are prime examples of the ways the habit cycle operates in social and work settings. The ways we attend, listen, pause, paraphrase, and inquire are all habits. However, unquestioned habits are often the reason for tension and lack of productivity in learning-focused relationships. For example, telling without asking, fixing not teaching, or solving a problem instead of facilitating problem-solving do not serve the goal of building capacity. It's important to explore whether a habit remains productive when contexts change. Automaticity with the learning-focused tool kit frees mental energy for greater responsiveness within growth-promoting conversations.

To break the habit cycle, a learning-focused supervisor needs three things: increased awareness of an existing habit, clarity of intention to build capacity, and a rich repertoire of communication tools. For example, a teacher approaches the supervisor with a problem (cue); the supervisor's present habit is to offer a solution; however, she recognizes this (awareness) and chooses to paraphrase and inquire (new routine); resulting in the satisfaction of supporting a more thoughtful, self-reliant approach to problem-solving for the teacher (new reward).

Figure 4.2 The Habit Cycle/Breaking the Habit Cycle

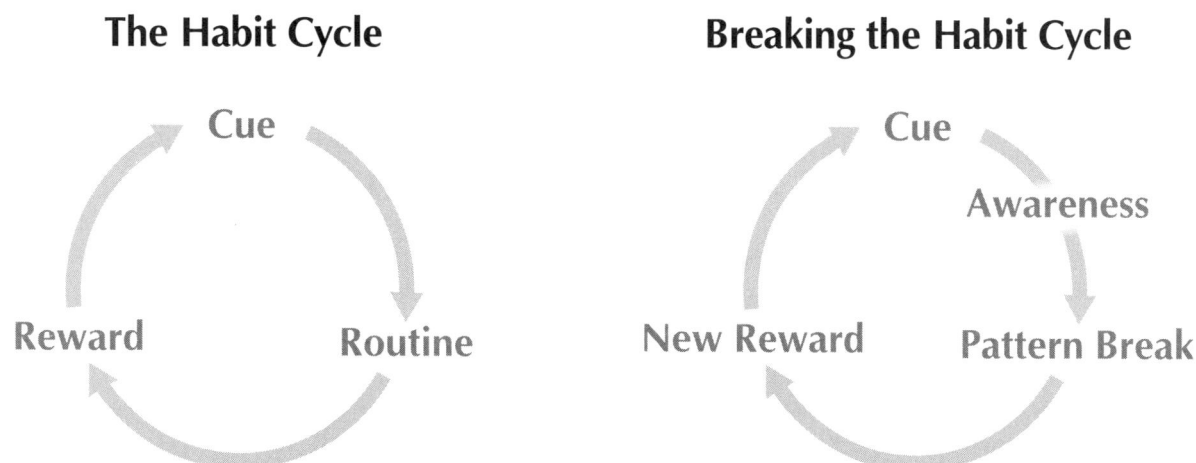

A stimulus in the environment (cue) flags consciousness about embedded routines (awareness); a new physical, mental, or emotional response replaces the old routine (pattern break); which results in the satisfaction of building capacity in others (new reward) that breaks the habit cycle.

Habits and the Brain

Being able to apply the tools in the Learning-Focused Tool Kit with grace and agility frees the supervisor's mental energy, allowing greater attention on the teacher and the issues being discussed. Learning these skills, or any new skills, and developing them into habits takes commitment, time, and repetition. Deliberate practice rewires the brain by developing new neural circuits which fire faster and consume less of the brain's energy.

When individuals who are learning a new skill are placed in an fMRI scanner, their brains show the most activity in the executive-control areas of the midbrain and prefrontal cortex. These regions are associated with self-control, planning, and abstract thought. In essence, learners are consciously thinking about the task and monitoring their actions. As the brain rewires through practice and repetition, fMRI scans display much less activity in the executive-control areas and increased activity in the sensorimotor loop in the deeper, less-conscious parts of the brain. The transition between these areas of the brain converts skills into habits. This neural shift marks the passage from novice to more expert practice for any new skill or set of skills. The growth of these new neural pathways drives the increase in skill enhancement and the ease and efficiency of performing the skill (Wood, 2019).

Attending Fully

Given the many demands of life in schools, being fully present with others is often a challenge for busy supervisors. Focusing complete attention on another person requires the emotional and mental discipline to shut out both external and internal distractions. You cannot fake listening. As a species, we have developed finely regulated systems for assessing and detecting when other people are paying attention to us. Babies learn to recognize and regulate their emotions based on their parents' reactions to their vocalizations, facial expressions, and other physical behaviors. Psychologists refer to this process as attunement. Well-attuned parents detect and reflect the baby's responses, creating a feedback loop that shapes the developing brain and strengthens the parent-infant bond. We carry this system of awareness within us as adults. Learning-focused conversations tap these resources when attentive supervisors align with and focus their energy on the teachers with whom they are interacting.

Threat Detection: Creating Conditions for Cognitive Challenge

The brain is wired to detect threats. Humans, like all animals, rapidly assess information in their environment for signs of danger. These signals, whether real or imagined, are fast-tracked on the brain's neural superhighways, taking priority over other, more thoughtful processes. Incoming signals from visual, auditory, and tactile circuits flow into the amygdala, an almond shaped structure located deep within the limbic system in the midbrain. The amygdala's essential task is to connect emotional content to memory. Both positive and negative emotional experiences affect this neural chemistry. The cortex, which holds higher level thinking structures, has more circuits running from the amygdala than to the amygdala.

Biologically, emotions drive thinking and attention, helping people to create meaning. For conversations to be learning-focused the teacher has to feel safe—thinking out loud requires risk-taking. Perception of threat occurs when the teacher's amygdala makes a rapid assessment of the body language, facial expressions, voice tone, and language choices of the supervisor. The molecules of emotion then hijack the brain/body system. The impression of threat inhibits processes, causing the teacher to shut down and revert to survival mode: freeze, fight, or flight.

Communicating Attention

At the most basic level, signaling full attention nonverbally aligns with the other person. Alignment has three distinct categories: physical elements, vocal elements, and breathing patterns.

Physical Elements

Physical elements include muscle tension, posture, and gesture. People who are aligned adopt similar postures with matching muscle tensions and reflect or borrow gestures from each other. Imagine you are in a restaurant, observing two people across the room. You can tell if they are relating well, even if you can't hear what they are saying. You might observe them leaning toward each other, nodding, smiling, and gesturing animatedly as they engage in conversation. They dance the dance of attunement as the talk shifts back and forth.

Attentive supervisors physically align their bodies with a teacher by sitting at a ninety-degree angle, ideally at the corner of a table, matching posture and physically paraphrasing the teacher's gestures. Physical barriers such as having a desk between the supervisor and teacher tend to interfere with alignment, producing both physical and emotional distance.

Vocal Elements

Vocal elements include intonation, pacing, and word choice. Humans are wired to appropriate the vocal patterns of those around them. By living and working in close proximity to others, we develop shared accents, speech patterns, and vocabularies. When traveling to other parts of the world, we tend to notice the vocal patterns of local people, especially when they are different from our home region. This same type of vocal alignment occurs within professions when practitioners develop and use lexicons and jargons.

By consciously noting and reflecting the patterns of others, adept supervisors first match and then modulate the conversation to connect emotionally and increase understanding. The supervisor can then carefully adjust the tone, pace, and language of the conversation to increase psychological safety, thoughtfulness, and learning opportunities.

Breathing Patterns

Breathing patterns include depth, duration, and rate. When humans align, they match breathing patterns. This occurs across a range of emotions. Breath is shallow and fast when someone is upset and more deep and slow when relaxed. These respiration patterns are linked to muscle tension as a part of the physical systems linked to emotional responses. A common experience for parents when reading at bedtime is to unconsciously match the breathing pattern of the child, and as the little one nods off the parent also gets drowsy.

Learning-focused supervisors note the breathing patterns of teachers with whom they interact. Matching posture and muscle tension tends to produce a match in depth, duration, and rate of breathing. Thinking brains consume a great deal of oxygen. Deeper breathing produces the needed energy for these processes.

Learning-Focused Supervision

Attunement and Alignment

Engaging fully in thoughtful and sometimes difficult explorations of teaching and learning issues requires teachers to draw upon both physical and emotional resources. Skilled supervisors anticipate when to be especially attentive to the need for attunement and alignment. These occasions include times when:

- **Tension or anxiety is anticipated or emerges within the conversation.** For example, no matter how positive the relationship between a supervisor and teacher, there is likely to be some anxiety when engaging in a reflecting conversation about a classroom observation or when reviewing a lesson plan together.
- **There is difficulty understanding another person.** Sometimes it feels like people are operating on different wavelengths. When miscommunication occurs, purposeful realignment and matching a colleague physically is often an effective strategy for reengaging and increasing comprehension of the other person's ideas.
- **Someone is distracted or having difficulty paying attention.** So often, the limited time to meet with a teacher is "borrowed" from time that could be devoted to other tasks. Sometimes it is difficult to keep these tasks, both personal and professional, from diverting the conversation. In such cases, intentional monitoring for alignment keeps attention fully on colleagues.

Implications & Applications: Attending Fully

Implications

The ability to be fully present and offer full attention is essential in building learning-focused supervisory relationships. Inattention to behaviors can hinder or block interpersonal and intellectual connection making.

1. What are some of your personal distractions that interfere with being fully present with teachers during supervisory interactions?
2. What are some cases where you need to be especially mindful of being fully present during supervisory interactions?

Applications

1. In informal settings, practice attending fully and note the effects on the conversation.
2. When you are planning for more formal conversation, remind yourself to physically align with the teacher when you sit down together.

Listening to Understand

Attentive listening is a full body experience, requiring our complete focus on the other person and noticing and managing any inner responses which may distract from the information and meaning the other person is trying to convey. The English word *listen* has roots associated with the words *ear* and to *lean* or to *list*. When listening carefully, we literally give ear to another by leaning or listing physically and emotionally in the direction of the speaker.

Section 4: A Learning-Focused Tool Kit

Four Blocks to Understanding

Four common internal distractions—listening habits—inhibit effective listening. These blocks to understanding shift our listening focus inward to our own opinions, interests, or surety about solutions. For learning-focused supervisors, it is particularly important to maintain awareness and listening discipline because listening from our own worldview diminishes the capacity to understand a teacher's perceptions and concerns. In many ways, listening limitations—blocks to understanding—are "self-centered" forms of listening, with a focus inwardly on ourselves and not outwardly on our conversation partner. Learning-focused supervisors are "other-minded."

Personal Listening

Personal listening inspires "me too" or "I would never" responses, whether internal or spoken aloud. This occurs when someone's mind shifts from listening to understand another to considering what is said with reference to our own experiences and judging its worth. Personal listening often leads to judgmental responses or personal anecdotes. Brief examples from the supervisor's own experiences may be appropriate to build the relationship and show empathy. However, there is a fine line between those intentions and making the supervisor's story or personal perspective the focus of the conversation.

With personal listening, the potential message to the teacher is that the supervisor's perspective, experience, and knowledge is more important than the teacher's thinking.

Detail Listening

Detail listening drives attention when there is a concern that the specifics might not be in place, and then leads to inquiring to ensure that they are. This listening may be triggered when the supervisor feels the need to have the complete picture to support the teacher. For example, detail listening produces questions like, "What type of container will you use for each group's art supplies?" These questions tend to stimulate recall of inconsequential information rather than lead to more complex thinking.

With detail listening, the potential message to teachers is mistrust in their thinking abilities or that important logistics might not be in place unless the supervisor inquires about them.

Predictive Listening

Predictive listening is listening *for* something rather than *to* someone. This block happens when someone listens for what they expect to hear while

---

BLOCKS TO UNDERSTANDING
- Personal listening
- Detail listening
- Predictive listening
- Certainty listening

Typical speaking rate:
125 to 150 words per minute

Typical listening rate:
500 to 800 words per minute

Listening versus Speaking Rates

Listening without formulating internal judgments and responses takes practice and discipline. Normal speaking rate is about 125 to 150 words per minute (Waks, 2010). Estimates of listening rates vary from 500 to 800 words per minute, meaning that humans can process speech at a higher rate than speakers can produce it. Most listeners internally fill this gap between speaking rate and processing rate with their own thoughts and judgments, and in doing so may miss essential information about the speaker's ideas, emotions, and current degree of understanding of the issues being considered.

Learning-Focused Supervision

filtering out what is actually said. Biases influence these predictions both negatively and positively. For example, generalizations about age, gender, ethnicity, attire, classroom organization, and personal belief systems can unintentionally affect expectations about a teacher's character, competence, and professionalism. Predictive listening begins before anything is said and leads to selecting or rejecting from among the actual messages expressed. This listening habit skews the conversation to a supervisor-driven focus rather than a teacher-driven focus.

With predictive listening, the potential message to the teacher is that the supervisor's assumptions and judgments should frame the conversation rather than the teacher's thinking or perspectives.

Certainty Listening

Certainty listening occurs when one is sure they know the solution to a problem, sometimes before listening carefully enough to ensure understanding of the teacher's perception about the problem. Before an issue is fully framed and mutually understood, this type of listening motivates offering advice or proposing solutions. Certainty listening may also trigger thinking queries that are forms of disguised advice such as "Have you tried?" or "Have you thought of?"

With certainty listening, the potential message to the teacher is that the supervisor has greater knowledge and expertise about the issue at hand, or that the supervisor's way is the right way.

*"The English word *listen* has roots associated with the words *ear* and to *lean* or to *list*. When listening carefully, we literally give ear to another by leaning or listing physically and emotionally in the direction of the speaker."*

Listening and the Habit Cycle

Removing or diminishing a block to understanding is a classic habit-cycle intervention. Addressing specific blocks requires awareness of listening routines and the cues that might trigger them.

Personal listening is cued when a teacher shares a story that resonates. The supervisor responds with their own story or example and is rewarded with a feeling of contributing to the conversation and the relationship, as well as the enjoyment of relating a bit of their own history.

Detail listening is cued when a teacher describes a plan or activity and the supervisor becomes curious about the specific elements that might be included. This form of listening triggers questions about particulars and misses opportunities to explore the bigger picture and the teacher's underlying thinking. In some cases, this listening and responding habit may communicate mistrust or doubt in the teacher's professional capacities.

Predictive listening is cued when the supervisor presumes to know what the teacher is going to say based on prior experiences with that person but based on very little information. This form of listening limits the possibilities for genuine exchange by cutting off the speaker before they have had a chance to fully express their ideas.

Certainty listening is cued when the solution in the supervisor's head overpowers the ability to listen to the teacher. This confidence in thinking and the need to share limits the opportunity to support the teacher's growth in decision-making and problem-solving skills.

With awareness of listening habits, one can interrupt these routines and break unproductive patterns by using new routines built on pausing, paraphrasing, and inquiring. These growth-promoting behaviors earn the reward of decreasing dependency and increasing the capacities of the teachers being supervised.

Giving full attention to a colleague contributes to relationship and to clear communication. These are the foundations for mutual learning and future exploration. Relationship and learning are intertwined both in the moment and over time. Learning and thinking draw upon person-to-person and person-to-idea connections. Subtle moves and behaviors nurture these relationships and desired thinking processes.

Implications & Applications: Listening to Understand

Implications

Purposeful listening signals a supervisor's respect for the teacher and a desire to understand fully before responding. Careful listening is the underpinning for offering paraphrases and inquiries that support teachers' thinking and increase the time efficiency of learning-focused conversations. Complete the listening survey available at: **go.SolutionTree.com/leadership**

1. What are some of your listening tendencies?
2. What cues might trigger non-productive listening?

Applications

1. In low-threat settings, such as social occasions or other casual conversations, notice your automatic responses to the conversational cues of those with whom you are interacting.
2. In these same settings, purposefully try out some new patterns of responses. Notice the results for the speaker and for you as a listener.
3. In supervisory settings, notice your automatic responses and try out some new patterns. Notice the results for the speaker and for you as a listener.

Pacing for Thoughtfulness: Using Purposeful Pauses

In our time-conscious culture, fast-paced conversations coupled with a lack of focused attention undermine teachers' confidence and their capacity to think energetically about the work of learning and teaching. Some people erroneously equate speed of response with higher degrees of intelligence. When supervisors do not adjust their pace to the thinking pace of the teacher with whom they are engaging, they may cut off developing thoughts or prematurely jump to consultation in an attempt to save their struggling colleague. Mindful supervisors always pause before rescue and often discover rescue is not needed.

Learning-Focused Supervision

The pace of a conversation affects both the emotional and intellectual climate. Frequent, well-placed pauses create and support a climate for thinking. For most people, however, consciously pausing to provide space for this thinking requires patience and practice. Silence can feel uncomfortable for both the listener and speaker unless there is a shared understanding that complex thinking takes and requires time.

Purposeful Pausing

Supervisors support teacher thinking when they strategically pause during learning-focused conversations. Science educator and researcher Mary Budd Rowe (1986) first noted the positive effects of pausing in the classroom. She labeled these pauses "Wait Time." Wait Time is the length of time we pause to allow thinking. Rowe suggests three to five seconds. More complex cognitive tasks may require a full five seconds or more.

In supervisory conversations, there are four critical junctures for pausing: after asking a question, after the teacher has offered initial thinking, before paraphrasing, and after a paraphrase.

- **Pause after asking a question.** This pause allows time and signals support for thinking. It communicates a belief in the teacher's capacity and willingness to think.
- **Pause after the teacher has offered initial thinking.** This pause allows the teacher to mentally retrieve additional and/or related information.
- **Pause before paraphrasing.** This pause allows the supervisor to fully absorb the teacher's communication and to construct an appropriate paraphrase.
- **Pause after a paraphrase.** This pause allows the teacher to confirm or correct the paraphrase and allows the supervisor to consider a strategic next move, which might include asking a question to move forward on the conversation template, to go deeper within the area of exploration, to inquire for detail, or to shift to another stance on the continuum.

Pausing as a Habit

Several factors inhibit people's ability to pause constructively. These include discomfort with silence, the misconception that pausing takes too much time, or feeling the need to have an answer and produce it quickly.

Understanding the importance of pausing to promote thinking and to honor teachers' information-processing styles motivates supervisors to better manage the pace of their conversations by making pausing a habit.

More productive routines start with awareness of pausing patterns and the effects on others, coupled with intentional use of wait time.

Pause Video
vimeo.com/miravia/pause

Implications & Applications: Purposeful Pausing

Implications

Purposefully pacing a conversation for thoughtfulness is a key factor in supporting learning, and yet it can be a challenging habit to cultivate.

1. What are some of your own pausing tendencies?
2. What cues might trigger discomfort with pausing?

Applications

1. In informal settings and during phone conversations, intentionally pause and note the effects for the people with whom you are interacting.
2. Monitor your own pausing patterns to identify the pausing forms you use the least. Purposefully develop new patterns by intentionally lengthening your pauses. Try counting silently to four or increase your acuity by attending to your partner's nonverbal signs. Note the results for others and for you as a listener.

Applying Verbal Tools

Language and thinking are interactive processes. Each energizes the other. Each limits the other. The language choices supervisors make influence a teacher's readiness, confidence, and ability to think. These strategic decisions shape expectations for the supervisory process and the working relationship. Thought-filled conversations combine nonverbal skills with the verbal tools of paraphrasing and inquiring.

This blend of tools affects the teacher's emotions and cognition. Learning-focused supervision is a developmental, growth-oriented model. As such, language that communicates the supervisor's belief in the teacher's motivation to continuously improve and their ability to do so is critical. Word choice can stimulate both positive and negative responses. These subtle messages embedded in communication are called presuppositions (see Positive Presuppositions, p. 76).

Entering the Teacher's World: Using Paraphrase

A paraphrase is a response that reflects the meaning, or understood meaning, of a speaker by using different words to summarize and increase clarity. In learning-focused conversations, the purposeful use of paraphrase produces several positive results, including:

- signaling that your colleague has your full attention;
- communicating a desire to understand the teacher's thoughts, concerns, questions, and ideas, as well as the importance of the teacher as a colleague; and
- providing a launching point to connect whatever follows, such as a question or suggestion, to the initial speaker's context or concern.

Learning-Focused Supervision

Effective paraphrases align the speaker and responder, establish understanding, and communicate regard. With this foundation, you earn permission to inquire for details, press for elaboration, or offer your own perspective or ideas. Without the paraphrase, inquiries can be perceived as interrogation, and suggestions can be perceived as impositions.

Well-crafted paraphrases influence both relationship and cognition. The paraphrase reflects a speaker's thinking back to the speaker for further consideration, connecting the speaker and the listener in a flow of discourse. Combined with appropriate pauses, paraphrases trigger more thoughtful responses than questions alone.

FOUR DO'S OF PARAPHRASE

- Avoid personal pronouns: "It seems to me...", "What I hear you saying..."
- Less is more: Keep the response shorter than the initiating statement
- Wait until the speaker is finished: Listen without interruption before paraphrasing
- Use tone to communicate intention: Invite confirmation or correction using an approachable voice

> "Without the paraphrase, inquiries can be perceived as interrogation, and suggestions can be perceived as impositions."

Three Types of Paraphrases with Three Intentions

Paraphrases label and reflect the speaker's content and often their emotions about the content. The ways in which this language is organized determines the type of paraphrase offered. Three different paraphrase types, with three different intentions, widen the range of possible responses for learning-focused supervisors. Versatility in use of paraphrase gives a skillful supervisor a wide range of actions from which to choose.

The three types, or paraphrase categories, are Acknowledge and Clarify, Summarize and Organize, and Shift Level of Abstraction. Each has a different but related purpose. There is no formula for which paraphrase type to use in any given instance. The skilled supervisor attends fully to both nonverbal and verbal cues from the teacher and chooses accordingly.

Acknowledge and Clarify

Acknowledge and clarify paraphrases provide an opportunity to identify and directly reflect content and emotions by restating the essence of someone's statements. The language in this paraphrase type is, essentially, on the same level of abstraction as the initial statement. By design, these paraphrases communicate our desire to understand and our value for the person and what they are feeling and saying. (Notice the intentional elimination of the personal pronoun "I" in the paraphrase examples that follow.)

> T: "I don't know how I'll get all of this work done. I've got a final exam to correct, end-of-term grades, and then the paperwork for closing the year!"
>
> S: "So you're concerned about successfully completing the key end-of-year tasks in what feels like a very limited amount of time."

Summarize and Organize

Summarize and organize paraphrases offer themes and containers which shape the initiating statement or separate jumbled issues. This type of paraphrase is useful when there's been a great deal said in a long stream of language.

Acknowledge and Clarify Paraphrase Video
vimeo.com/miravia/acknowledge

Summarize and Organize Paraphrase Video
vimeo.com/miravia/summarize

This type of paraphrase captures key elements and offers some organization to which the speaker can react. It provides a "shape" to the initiating statement. These organizing options include containers or categories, compare/contrast, large themes, or a sequence or hierarchy.

For example, consider the following.

> **T:** "There are a number of key skills I know my students need to be successful with the new curriculum, and I'm not sure if they are ready or if I have the instructional strategies for teaching them effectively."
>
> **S:** "It seems there are several things on your mind, right now: identifying the explicit skills needed for success with the curriculum change, getting your students ready to be successful, and enhancing your own repertoire to ensure their success." (identifying containers)
>
> **T:** "I'm so confused. During language arts, my students work well in groups, participate in class, and complete their assignments. In science, they are constantly off task, and I need to keep them doing individual work to keep control in the classroom."
>
> **S:** "You're noticing significant differences between your students' performance in language arts and their performance in science." (compare/contrast)
>
> **T:** "This teaching performance rubric clarifies expectations about classroom instruction and management as well as planning for effective teaching and ways to communicate and be professionally responsible in the school and community."
>
> **S:** "So you're noting that high expectations for professional practice include both active classroom practice as well as performance outside the classroom." (themes)
>
> **T:** "I'm thinking about setting up centers in my classroom, and I also want to use some formative assessments, and I'm not sure that my first graders are ready for the self-management needed to function in learning centers."
>
> **S:** "Your sense is that, given your interest in establishing learning centers, you might first need to assess the behavioral skills needed for self-guided work, then determine which skills to teach and to whom, then establish centers that will be effective for the different levels of readiness." (sequence/hierarchy)

Shifting Level of Abstraction

The Shifting Level of Abstraction paraphrase reflects the speaker's language more globally by shifting up, or more specifically by shifting down. These language shifts in turn influence the teacher's thinking. The intention of shifting up is to illuminate large ideas or categories, often leading the speaker to new discoveries, exploring potentially broad applications, or determining possibilities for transfer. The shift-down paraphrase increases precision of thought and clarifies understanding for both speaker and listener.

When the conversation enters abstract territory or for individuals who think in highly global patterns, the shift-down paraphrase is a way of grounding thinking with specific examples and details. This in turn encourages the teacher to contribute additional descriptions and examples. For individuals who tend to think or speak in highly sequential and concrete patterns,

Shift Level of Abstraction UP Paraphrase Video
vimeo.com/miravia/shiftup

Shift Level of Abstraction DOWN Paraphrase Video
vimeo.com/miravia/shiftdown

shifting up opens a broader vista for exploration and provides a wider context for the topics at hand.

Supervisors generally move to higher levels of abstraction by naming the big ideas including concepts, categories, goals, and values. Supervisors move to lower levels of abstraction when concepts need grounding, offering specific examples or pertinent details.

For example, consider the following.

> T: "My kids have trouble getting started, and they're always asking for help."
>
> S: "So you want your students to be more self-reliant." (shift up)
>
> or
>
> S: "For example, you're finding that your students seem to be having trouble following directions." (shift down)

A paraphrase that shifts to a higher level of abstraction is particularly effective in problem-solving situations. Initially, more abstract language widens the potential solution set and encourages broader exploration of ideas and strategies for problem-solving.

> T: "This math text is much too difficult for many of my students."
>
> S: "So you're looking for instructional materials that meet the needs of all of your students."

This shift-up paraphrase of math text to instructional materials opens the conversation to consider a wider range of solutions to this teacher's concern.

Paraphrase as a Habit

Using a paraphrase creates a safe space for a thoughtful working relationship. When paraphrase is not applied consistently, conversations can feel rushed and brusque. Teachers may not feel valued or understood and may form the perception that the supervisor's agenda, not their issues or concerns, matter most.

> **EXPERT MOVE**
>
> Expert supervisors routinely make paraphrase a first response when talking with teachers, rather than jumping immediately to problem-solving or advice giving. This habit allows them to be fully present with the teacher, listen at deep levels to presenting issues, and respond as needed with inquiries or consultative information.

Paraphrase and Problem-Solving

In the hectic world of schools, time is a scarce commodity. Stopping to consider and frame issues productively often goes by the wayside in a frenzied environment. Sometimes everything seems equally urgent. As a result, during problem-solving conversations, supervisors may find themselves interacting with teachers who are by degrees confused, overwhelmed, or reacting with strong feelings to an event or issue. At these times, teachers and supervisors are often at their least flexible. Skillful and well-timed paraphrasing offers access to emotional resources, which increases readiness for addressing pressing issues.

A Scaffold for Crafting Paraphrases

Acknowledge and Clarify

- So, you're feeling _____
- You're noticing that _____
- In other words _____
- You're suggesting that _____

Summarize and Organize

- So, there seem to be two key issues here _____ and _____
- On the one hand, there is _____ and on the other hand, there is _____
- For you then, several themes are emerging; _____
- It seems you're considering a sequence or hierarchy here; _____

Shift Level of Abstraction (Up)

- So, a(n) _____ for you might be _____
  - concept · assumption
  - value/belief
  - goal · intention

Shift Level of Abstraction (Down)

- So, a(n) _____ for you might be _____
  - example · non-example

The human brain/body system does not make distinctions between feeling and thinking. As described earlier, biochemically, humans are one interconnected and interacting mix of molecules regulating hormonal responses and the production or suppression of the neurotransmitters that support higher-level thinking. The molecules of emotion and the molecules of cognition respond in the moment to the influences of thoughtful interaction. At times like these, attentive supervisors strategically apply specific types of paraphrases to support the emotional and mental resourcefulness of their teachers.

The goal paraphrase is especially effective in this regard. A goal paraphrase usually shifts the level of abstraction up and works to illuminate potential outcomes. Often, when a goal becomes "visible," emotional resourcefulness returns and the intellectual readiness for problem-solving emerges. Goal paraphrases are an important first step in problem-solving conversations. They set the stage for the inquiries that follow (see Figure 3.3 Learning-Focused Conversations: A Template for Problem-Solving).

Well-Formed Goal Paraphrases

By attending fully to others and aligning physically, supervisors create the first level of psychological safety necessary for successful problem-solving conversations. This skill couples with careful listening at multiple levels to the "story" being presented and to the "story beneath the story." Goal paraphrases are built on listening to what's beneath the story. Skillful supervisors are mindful that the listening blocks to understanding (personal, detail, predictive, and certainty) inhibit the ability to produce this level of understanding. Goal paraphrases raise the level of abstraction of the initiating issue making desired outcomes broadly visible and widening the solution set to increase problem-solving options.

Consider the following.

> **T:** "Some of my afternoon lab groups are unruly and have difficulty focusing on tasks and learning material. They fool around for most of the period, and then there's a mad rush to fill out lab sheets at the end. All the attention is on completing the sheet and not on the processes of learning how to do science."
>
> **S:** "So you want to feel confident that your students' energy is engaged in learning science process in your lab, not just doing the required worksheets."

Head nods, postural shifts, changes in muscle tension, and/or verbal responses are external cues that indicate internal shifts. By carefully monitoring these subtle signals, an alert supervisor recognizes when a proposed goal seems to fit for the teacher. Goal paraphrases offer a glimpse of a potential positive future. In this way, they provide an orientation that psychologically removes the other person from the muddle of the moment. When these possibilities align with the listener's context, related biochemical changes provide the necessary emotional and cognitive resources for problem-solving.

Once the broad goal is established—for example, "You want to feel respected by your colleagues"—the subsequent conversation works to clarify and define vague language. For example, the supervisor might ask, "What are

Learning-Focused Supervision

some specific examples of respect?" When the desired outcome is clear, it is more likely that the teacher is ready to consider potential actions for achieving this goal.

Verbal and Nonverbal Referencing

Gestural language and verbal language are linked systems. In problem-solving conversations, the gestural vocabulary carries information that amplifies and extends the verbal portions. In some cases, the body knows more than the mouth or knows it before language is constructed to convey the message.

Attention to nonverbal messages increases the effectiveness and efficiency of communication. The subtle cues that are given and received maximize the clarity of the information and lead to greater productivity for both parties in the conversation. Aware supervisors attend to the teacher's vocal patterns, such as rhythm, pitch, and pace, that indicate changes in thinking or feeling; they consider intonation, emphasis, and volume as cues to what might be important or of primary concern in the narrative. Similarly, lengthy pauses, sighs, and repetition also provide meaningful signals.

Speakers place characters in space. It is useful to note how near, on which side, and where the characters are in relation to each other. Speakers also place concepts in space. These are sometimes grouped and compared or contrasted nonverbally as the story details unfold. Time orientations are another form of gesture, for example, a hand from back to front or left to right indicating past, present, and future. Gestural emphasis and patterns indicate a sequence or hierarchy of ideas or actions and give information about what might not be being said aloud, but what might still matter to the speaker.

Gestures with Paraphrase

Human nonverbal communication patterns are as rich and distinctive as spoken language. People have unique external cues to internal thinking processes. While the patterns might be idiosyncratic, there are some useful generalizations. For example, handedness plays a part in these patterns. Discerning hand dominance and observing marker cues is a useful communication tool. By noting where in space a speaker places story elements and characters, we can paraphrase both nonverbally and verbally by referencing these locations with our own gestures. Attentive supervisors watch for signs of cross-lateralization. The shift from left to right or right to left indicates shifts across the corpus callosum, the membrane that connects the brain's hemispheres. These shifts are external signs of brain integration and increasing efficacy towards problem solution.

PHYSICAL REFERENCING

- Characters in space
- Concepts in space
- Sequence or hierarchy
- Time orientation

Physical Referencing Video
vimeo.com/miravia/referencing

Marker Language	Marker Gestures
Verbal Stress • Volume • Emphasis • Repetition • Pace • Referencing	Physical Stress • Volume • Emphasis • Repetition • Pace • Referencing

Section 4: A Learning-Focused Tool Kit

Physical referencing is a subtle but powerful skill that communicates understanding, increases psychological safety, and mediates thinking. By paying attention to these elements as they are communicated and continuing to develop increased acuity, an observant supervisor facilitates communication and accelerates learning.

Shifting Language, Shifting Thought: Levels of Abstraction

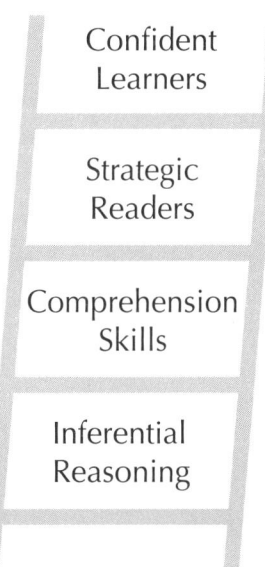

LADDER OF ABSTRACTION

Confident Learners

Strategic Readers

Comprehension Skills

Inferential Reasoning

Language is a system of agreed-upon labels. For example, English-speakers understand that the thing we sit around, set, and dine upon is a table. They also understand that the word *table* represents many types of this thing (coffee, dining, etc.), and that each of these labels also represent specific types: a coffee table might be round, rectangular, high, low, or of certain dimensions. Therefore, knowing a language means understanding not only words, but the words in relation to the things (categories) and actions that they represent. When someone hears or says the word *table*, they may think of a particular item and simultaneously understand the subsets that the word represents, as well as the idea that the word itself is a subset—of furniture, for example. Linguist S. I. Hayakawa (1964) describes these levels of language as a ladder of abstraction.

For skillful communicators, this concept suggests that all language resides at some level of abstraction. As described above, *table* is an abstraction of all the types of tables. Abstractions, both mentally and linguistically, eliminate differences between things. This relabeling is an indispensable aid to thoughtful and clear communication. When it is desirable to discuss broad themes and concepts, shifting up the ladder of abstraction allows for generalizations. For example, the paraphrase, "So you're looking for dining-room furniture" might move the conversation beyond a discussion about tables. By drilling down—exploring lower levels of abstraction—speaker and listener increase clarity about the topic of discussion. For example, the question, "When you say *table*, what are some of the qualities you are considering?" would likely produce a response that establishes specific parameters, dimensions, and qualities.

Levels of Abstraction in Learning-Focused Conversations

Defining is not the same as knowing. For example, a classroom teacher might be able to clearly define guided reading, but that doesn't mean they know how to produce an effective guided reading lesson or even recognize one being taught. If the supervisor's intention is to ground the conversation in specifics about the qualities of guided-reading lessons and applying these qualities within the context of a specific classroom or curriculum, then the exchange would be well served by staying at lower levels of abstraction, at least initially. However, at some point, to effectively move beyond a single or highly specific context, for transfer and broader applications, higher levels of abstraction would be desirable and necessary.

Consider the following interaction. Note that in this conversation, with attention to levels of abstraction, both paraphrase and inquiry are applied to refine a general goal (e.g., do more with guided reading) into a measurable outcome. Both positive presuppositions and levels of abstraction are

Learning-Focused Supervision

embedded in these verbal tools to increase thoughtfulness by building confidence, offering choice, and defining vague areas.

T: "One goal for me this year is to do more with guided reading."

S: "So you're interested in adding to your present instructional approaches. Given what you know about your students, what are some things that led you to choosing guided reading?"

T: "Well, I know that guided reading is done with small groups, and that it is effective in producing more strategic readers. I already work with my kids in groups, and they're used to that."

S: "One advantage, then, is that you can capitalize on your students' readiness to work in groups. What are some reading skills you feel would be important at this point in the school year?"

T: "Well, they definitely need to strengthen their literal comprehension skills and their use of context clues, firm up sound/symbol relationships, especially consonant and vowel blends, and for some of them, work on word structure, like syllabication and compound words."

S: "So your goal is to have an array of reading strategies to build into your instruction, leading to greater student success. As you consider using guided reading to do so, what kinds of assessments are you planning to determine their success and yours?"

Implications & Applications: The Power of Paraphrasing

Implications

Paraphrase is an essential resource for building and sustaining learning-focused relationships by creating a safe environment for thinking. Paraphrase communicates receptivity and the desire to understand the speaker without judgment.

1. Under what conditions do you choose to paraphrase (or choose not to paraphrase)?
2. How often do you paraphrase using formulaic language, such as, "What I hear you saying" or "I think I hear you saying that"?

Applications

1. Use the paraphrase scaffolds (see sidebar p. 68) to support your construction of paraphrases and eliminate the use of the pronoun "I."
2. Set a goal for increasing your confidence and fluency with each type of paraphrase. Isolate the skill (e.g., focus on paraphrasing in social or casual professional conversations) to make each type of paraphrase automatic.
3. Pay attention to the length of your paraphrases. Be sure they are shorter than the initiating statement.

Invitational Inquiry

Artful question construction is a powerful and learnable skill that combines with skillful pausing and paraphrasing to increase the learning potential of supervisory conversations. For many supervisors, thinking about inquiry in the context of learning-focused conversations requires a shift in intention. For thoughtful supervisors, inquiry is not about gathering information. The goal of inquiry is to produce thinking and to help the teacher integrate the self-talk of expertise. As a result, effective inquiries reflect this internal dialogue and make it accessible to all practitioners.

Compare the following questions in the context of a planning conversation.

"In this interactive lesson, what size will the groups be?"

versus

"In interactive lessons, what are some criteria you use to determine group size?" (And then perhaps, "How are you applying those criteria to this lesson/class?")

Here is another example, in the context of a reflecting conversation.

"These data indicate that you stayed in front of the class for 90 percent of the instructional time. What are some reasons you limited your movement?"

versus

"These data indicate that you stayed in front of the class for 90 percent of the instructional time. What are some ways you monitor and choose where you position yourself in the classroom?"

Note that in the first response in each example, the supervisor is essentially gathering information. In the second response, the supervisor inquires about the teacher's thinking and ideally offers questions that the teacher will continue to ask herself when planning or reflecting upon instruction. In addition, these thought-provoking questions are more likely to produce guiding generalizations. This concept that inquiry is first and foremost about increasing a teacher's ability for learning about and from their practice is fundamental to the supervisory process.

> "This concept that inquiry is first and foremost about increasing a teacher's ability for learning about and from their practice is fundamental to the supervisory process."

Designing Questions to Promote Thinking

Growth-promoting supervisors are purposeful in their use of questions. A supervisor's linguistic repertoire includes the capacity to construct inquiries that clarify and stimulate complexity of thinking. These questions communicate a spirit of curiosity and a desire to explore information and ideas.

Questions that clarify thinking harvest multiple responses, and also probe for increased specificity of information. These questions elicit examples, criteria, and details that support precision in verbal responses and greater precision in thinking. Questions that stimulate complex thinking invite responses that offer multiple and expanded ideas and thoughts. These questions elicit concepts, categories, and generalizations. Both types of questions are an important part of the learning-focused supervisor's repertoire. Well-crafted questions contain nonverbal and verbal elements that invite thinking.

Learning-Focused Supervision

Creating the Conditions for Thinking

To respond thoughtfully to rich and purposeful inquiry requires emotional readiness on a teacher's part. The full array of nonverbal and verbal skills is in use here. Purposeful paraphrasing creates this readiness. It works in concert with the nonverbal skills described above and fits within a pattern that paces the conversation for thinking, interspersing functional pauses before and after paraphrasing and inquiring. Inquiry delves into what is not yet known, or not readily available. Thus, it is necessary for the teacher to be willing to deal with the discomfort of not knowing and to be open to discovery during the supervisory exchange.

Questions that extend and illuminate thinking invite a wide range of potential responses. Inviting thinking begins with eliciting these verbal responses. Once surfaced, language and thinking can always be honed and refined. But without them, there is little with which to work. Well-crafted inquiries integrate three essential elements: offering an invitation to engage, naming a cognitive process, and determining a topic. These elements can be combined in a variety of ways and do not always appear in a fixed order; their interplay creates the emotional and cognitive context for engagement. By definition, inquiries do not have a preferred response. If you're confident there is a certain correct answer, don't ask a question—offer your thinking instead.

PATTERN OF DISCOURSE
listen/
pause/
paraphrase/
pause/
inquire

Template for Inquiry

Effective inquiries signal the supervisor's desire to explore ideas and communicate belief in the teacher's capacity, readiness, and willingness to think out loud. A blend of tonal and linguistic elements shapes well-crafted inquiries. This section describes the three interchangeable components: an invitation to engage, a cognitive focus, and a topic.

Figure 4.3 The Components of Inquiry

The Invitation

The invitation to think functions as a total package that wraps around communication. This invitation begins with clear signals that someone's full presence is available for this conversation and that no harm is intended. This invitation has two primary layers: tonal and syntactical. Listeners automatically assess the tone of the words they hear for any signs of threat (see Threat Detection, p. 58). This rapidly firing safety assessment influences both what is heard and how the incoming information is processed.

Elements of the Invitation Video
vimeo.com/miravia/elements

Section 4: A Learning-Focused Tool Kit

Interpreting the syntactical structure of the message is the next filtering system in the human brain. People analyze linguistic messages for both the type of response requested and for the degree of psychological safety that ultimately determines how forthcoming they are with answers.

The Tonal Layer

An approachable voice for framing language in a nonthreatening manner creates the tonal layer in the invitation (Grinder, 1997). An approachable voice is well modulated and rhythmic, with the tone rising at the end of the question. This vocal pattern signals a sense of openness and exploration that the teacher interprets as a request for participation. This intonation contrasts with the credible voice, which is more evenly modulated with a flatter tone and drops at the end of a statement. This voice pattern indicates that the speaker is sharing information and expertise. Voice choice signals the stance within which we are operating. The more approachable voice indicates a collaborating or coaching stance; the more credible voice indicates a calibrating or consulting stance.

The Syntactical Layer

Syntactical choices influence the way teachers respond to questions. These subtle elements encourage or inhibit thinking and influence the quality of the teacher's answers. Four key syntactical choices increase a teacher's emotional resources and expand the options for thinking: plural forms, exploratory language, nondichotomous forms, and positive presuppositions.

As described above, full attention and presence with the use of an approachable voice establishes the environment for emotionally safe and thoughtful conversations. These nonverbal elements combine with the following syntactical elements to create cognitively rich inquiries.

Plural Forms. Plural forms indicate that there are multiple possible responses. For example, *goals* instead of *goal*, *concerns* rather than *concern*. Combined with an approachable intonation, this pattern suggests that all responses at this point have merit, and that frees the teacher from having to evaluate and sort.

Exploratory Language. Exploratory language has a tentative quality. Examples include words like *some, might, seems, possible,* and *hunch*. These terms, like the use of plurals, widen the potential range of response and reduce the need for surety. Words like *could* and *why* tend to decrease the confidence of teachers who may interpret these words as questioning their capabilities for thought or indicate the need to justify their choices and actions. In addition, the word *could,* as in the question, "Given this issue, what could you do about it?" may interrupt thought processes by seeming to require a commitment to ideas or actions that the teacher is not yet ready to make. The use of *why* in an inquiry requires the responder to explain or defend their thinking. Further, the connotation is that the teacher needs to explain or defend their response to the supervisor.

Consider these examples.

> "What is the best way you could meet these students' learning needs?"
>
> *versus*

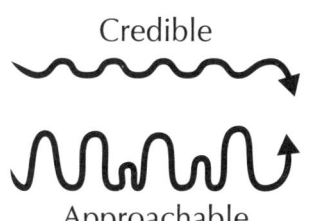

Approachable Voice Video
vimeo.com/miravia/approachable

Credible Voice Video
vimeo.com/miravia/credible

Six Elements of the Invitation

- Attending Fully
- Approachable Voice
- Plural Forms
- Exploratory Language
- Nondichotomous Forms
- Positive Presuppositions

Learning-Focused Supervision

"What might be some ways to address these students' learning needs?"

or

"Why did you use that example at that point in the lesson?"

versus

"What were some reasons for offering that example at that point in the lesson?"

Nondichotomous Forms. Another syntactical component of the invitation is the use of nondichotomous forms of a question. Dichotomous questions are those that can be answered yes or no, true or false, is or is not. In contrast, questions that invite thinking are framed with open-ended, nondichotomous forms. For example, instead of asking "Did you notice any unusual behaviors?" ask "What are some of the behaviors you noticed?" When we use dichotomous forms, we communicate doubt in capacity. For example, "Have you thought about these data as you plan for next week's instruction?" might suggest the supervisor's doubt that the data have been incorporated or are considered in planning on a consistent basis. Contrast that with, "What are some ways that these data are influencing your planning for next week's instruction?"

By eliminating dichotomous stems such as "Can you," "Did you," "Will you," or "Have you," we invite thinking and communicate positive presuppositions about the teacher's capacity and willingness to think.

Positive Presuppositions. All language expresses a supervisor's presuppositions about a teacher's professional abilities. Our brains are wired to discern the embedded presupposition in verbal messages. Negative presuppositions inhibit thinking, while positive presuppositions stimulate it (Elgin, 2000). Skilled supervisors purposefully communicate positive presuppositions when working with their teachers.

For example, contrast the following.

"Can you think of any ways to improve your classroom management?"

versus

"Given the important connections between student learning and a well-managed classroom, what are some routines you are implementing?"

or

"Do you see any ways that this student's work aligns with the writing rubric and meets expectations for written expression?"

versus

"As you compare this student's writing to the rubric descriptors, what are some areas of alignment with the expectations for written expression that you notice?"

While both inquiries are open-ended, the first examples question the capabilities of the teacher by communicating doubt in the teacher's awareness and ability to address the topic. The second examples express belief in the teacher's active and ongoing engagement with the topic.

SYNTACTICAL SUBSTITUTIONS

- the — some
- is/are — seems
- can/could — might
- why — what

STEMS TO CONVEY POSITIVE PRESUPPOSITIONS

- Given your knowledge of...
- Based on your experience with...
- Reflecting on...
- As you consider...

Section 4: A Learning-Focused Tool Kit

Cognition: Stimulating and Clarifying Thinking

Skillful teaching is cognitively demanding. Expertise requires drawing on personal knowledge and present experience, processing and integrating information, and constructing new ideas and applications. This level of professional practice demands moving from more simple cognitive operations, like recollection and description, to more complex thinking, like analysis and inference making, then moving to novel constructions for designing instructional approaches and adaptations to student learning needs.

For example, planning identifies learning needs, then envisions clear outcomes, then designs applications. Reflecting supports recollection of experience, then analysis of results, then integration of new understandings. Problem-solving clarifies salient factors, then prioritizes causal factors, and finally formulates possible solutions.

Learning-focused supervisors craft inquiries that are purposefully driven by clear cognitive intentions. The effectiveness and efficiency of planning, reflecting, and problem-solving is amplified by targeting specific thinking processes. Questions that invite and focus thinking build professional capacity and self-directed learning. Embedded within each phase of the Conversation Templates described in Section Three are verbs that promote specific cognitive processes. For example, teachers develop expertise in planning by identifying, predicting, and sequencing. Similarly, teachers make sense of experience when reflecting by inferring, comparing, and analyzing cause and effect. Knowledge is constructed when teachers generalize, hypothesize, apply, and synthesize. Effective problem-solving employs ways of thinking from both planning and reflecting.

By naming the cognitive focus, skilled supervisors exercise and develop the thinking processes used by expert teachers as they transfer the supervisor's questions into their self-talk. In addition, any topic can be explored in different ways depending on the cognitive focus embedded in the question.

Notice the difference among the following.

> "What are some ways you're thinking about classroom management?"
>
> or
>
> "How might you compare your classroom management this month to last month?"
>
> or
>
> "What might be some causes for the improvements you're noticing in classroom management this month?"

Question construction is a prime vehicle for supervisors to shape conversations that are customized and developmental. Naming the thinking process targets the internal search for information, easing both the emotional and cognitive load.

When the supervisor names the cognition required to respond to an inquiry, the efficiency of information retrieval increases. As in the example above, asking for comparisons facilitates thinking by focusing the search. Responsive supervisors customize their inquiries by making strategic adjustments during the flow of the conversation.

Implications & Applications: Invitational Inquiry

Implications

Attention to the intonation and syntax of inquiries increases the willingness of teachers to think aloud, especially when they lack confidence or are exploring an unresolved issue. Well-crafted inquiries eliminate the possibilities of a right/wrong dynamic and reduce the fear of judgment.

1. What are some of your inquiry patterns? What percentage of your inquiries are invitational?
2. What are some things you notice about the effects of your inquiries on the thinking of the teacher with whom you are interacting?

Applications

1. In low-threat settings, such as social events or casual conversations, monitor your use of dichotomous forms (yes/no or can you/have you/did you).
2. Make copies of the Inquiry Mat (see p. 86 or **go.SolutionTree.com/leadership**) and post them where you can see them. Use them as cues to remind you to apply these essential tools. Choose and overlearn one or two invitational stems, such as "What are some" and "How might you." Practice these inquiry starters in multiple settings.
3. When you prepare inquiries for staff and parent communications in formats such as emails, newsletters, and presentation slides, edit your questions by checking for invitational syntax and positive presuppositions.

Intention-Driven Questions: Inquiry to Clarify Thinking

There is much more information in an environment than ever appears in language. Brains filter incoming information and search for recognizable patterns. From these, people form meanings about the world and create mental models that shape and guide thinking and ultimately behavior. Human language reflects these thinking habits, resulting in surface vagueness that often masks or obscures the rich details that lie beneath.

For example, in describing a class, a teacher might simply say, "My students are really coming along with learning to cooperate." Beneath this surface statement is delight that students are following routines, working well in groups, being responsible for classroom materials, and are increasingly self-reliant. However, without inquiring for these details, that information is not available for exploration.

A Map is Not the Territory

Language is often like a trapdoor that obscures or hides what resides beneath it. All language has deeper attached meanings. Some of these meanings are known to the person speaking the words and some of these meanings remain hidden until teased into view.

Words are navigational markers to the map of the world. These maps are functional approximations of reality. They provide points of reference and the directional cues that shape our choices and behaviors. As semanticist Alfred Korzybski (1958) explained, "A map is not the territory it represents, but, if correct, it has a similar structure to the territory, which accounts for its usefulness…"

Inquiring for more specificity in a learning-focused conversation is important for several reasons. First, to be sure that there is a shared understanding, since what seems very clear to one party might be interpreted differently by the other. For example, the teacher implicitly defines "coming along with learning to cooperate" as the variety of details offered above. The supervisor might suppose she means that students are cooperating with the teacher, not necessarily with one another, and assume that they are listening to directions, handing in assignments, and adhering to classroom rules. Without inquiring, a very different take on the exchange and understanding of the teacher's perspective might result. These inquiries also serve to illuminate examples, details, and actions that define goals, increase clarity of thinking for the teacher, and may be critical to agreed-upon professional development plans.

In addition, by focusing on and clarifying specifics, an astute supervisor can help shift a situation from one that might feel overwhelming to one that is more manageable emotionally, physically, and intellectually. Like many supervisory skills, inquiring for specificity is based on listening. In this case, the skill set is listening for vague language and then deciding which terms, if clarified, would support the most productive shifts in thinking. For a clearer idea of what might produce vague language, it is important to understand the internal processes that produce it.

Deletions and Generalizations

Human brains create and are created by models of reality built from experiences in the world and from interpretations of those experiences. As a result, internal processes shape what appears in surface language: among these are deletions and generalizations (Bandler & Grinder, 1971). We delete incoming and outgoing data to fit deeply embedded mental templates. We generalize as a kind of short cut to making sense of our experience. These processes are not conscious on the speaker's part.

Deletions and generalizations result in vague language. It is useful to understand these two categories as they become important listening lenses for the attuned supervisor who selects a focus for clarification, paraphrases the essential ideas, then inquires to increase specificity within target areas. In many cases, more than one category of vagueness occurs in the same statement. In all cases, the skillful supervisor applies the pattern of pause, paraphrase, and then inquire.

Deletions

We delete when we overlook or omit information, either incoming or outgoing. In spoken and written language these deletions appear as vague nouns, vague pronouns, and vague verbs. For example, the speaker omits the qualities of the verb *appreciate,* or the number of parents who help their students do homework, or the percentage of units that are effective in the curriculum.

Let's take another look at the example above: "My students are really coming along with learning to cooperate."

There are several deletions here, including the qualities of cooperation, with whom the students are cooperating, which specific students are improving and in what ways. By inquiring into any of these deletions, an attentive

Learning-Focused Supervision

supervisor increases clarity in the conversation and precision in thinking for the teacher. For example, the supervisor might ask, "What are some examples of cooperative student behaviors that you see at this point in the school year?"

For supervisors, careful listening helps to inform the construction of questions that will support precision. On a regular basis, one hears conversational exchanges that include "my students," "the class," "my fourth period," "classroom management," "student behavior," "technology," "culturally relevant materials," "the parents," "the administration," "central office" and a host of other unspecified nouns. For many teachers, someone named "they" causes most of the problems in their class or school. "We," "us," and "them" are other possible sources of concern and/or joy.

In a learning-focused conversation, if we hear a teacher say, "My students don't understand fractions," it is important to find out how many students are confused about fractions and what elements of fraction learning are most problematic to them. Without these essential details, the supervisor can't know where to target energy and attention within the problem-solving process. Narrowing the field of focus in this case might identify subsets of students with distinct learning needs that can be addressed systematically by the teacher.

Planning, reflecting, and problem-solving require specificity for targeted action and personal learning. The term "understand" in the example above is a prime example. Once it's been determined who has the problem, next is to clarify the goal of understanding. What does this teacher mean by "understanding," and how will students display their own "understanding"? With some teachers, these specifications may lead to unpacking their own understanding of fractions as well.

Teacher goal-setting is a particularly important area for clarifying action. Words like *plan, improve, design, modify, enhance,* and *prepare* are all examples of unspecified verbs that have little meaning without clarification and details.

Additional Deletions

Another common linguistic deletion is when the speaker omits the criteria that is the basis of a comparison or reference point for a comparison. For example, when a teacher says, "Today's lesson was much better," two queries might be productive: "In what ways was it better?" and/or "What was it better than?" Discovering the speaker's criteria for "better" is essential to knowing how to proceed with the conversation. Is this "better" a success to build on or are poorly understood factors at work here that leave this "better" a mystery? Other vague comparators are words like *best, larger, slower, more, less,* and *least*.

Learning-focused supervisors support teachers by helping them to specify their criteria and standards for comparison. This action supports rigor in planning and problem-solving, which leads to targeted action and measurable signs of success. When a teacher says, "I want students to get better results on my next quiz," a supervisor might respond by probing for the qualities that would define better results. For example, does the teacher mean a higher class average or some other improvements in student responses?

DELETIONS

Vague nouns: my students, the class, my fourth period, central office

Vague pronouns: they, we, them, us

Vague verbs: understand, appreciate, control, prepare, design

ADDITIONAL DELETIONS

Comparators: better, slower, more, least

Section 4: A Learning-Focused Tool Kit

We also often need to surface the missing reference or lost comparator. For example, was this lesson better than the *best* lesson the teacher has taught to date—or better than the *worst*? Our continued conversation would be quite different, depending upon the response.

Generalizations

Generalizations are the brain's way of efficiently cataloging experience by placing a value on it for later reference. Generalizations are useful because people rely on these judgments when making additional choices. For example, if someone's experience with liquid laundry detergent (perhaps even a specific brand) versus powder has been positive, they will look for liquid detergent when shopping and not need to stop and analyze the choice each time. However, people get into trouble when generalizations are made from too little experience or when periodic stops are omitted to consciously review present generalizations. For example, a teacher attends a workshop that does not meet his needs and forms the impression or creates a generalization that all professional development is ineffective based on one experience and therefore avoids seeking any additional learning opportunities.

GENERALIZATIONS
Rules:
"I have to"
"we should"

UNIVERSAL QUANTIFIERS
"you always"
"I never"
"everyone thinks"

Everyone has a set of rules that guide personal ways of perceiving and operating in the world. People are not always conscious of these internal codes, but they appear in language in things like, "I have to," "I must," "I can't," "I should have," or "I shouldn't have." Many times, these rules are generalized from little or no-longer-relevant experience. For example, if a teacher says, "I can't let my students work in teams because they won't get any work done," the supervisor needs to carefully paraphrase and explore the reasons beneath the statement. For example, "You have some concerns about group work. What are some of your assumptions about the skills and attitudes your students might need to get the most out of learning together?" Intonation matters greatly here. The supervisor's voice must be carefully modulated: nonthreatening intonation is key to creating a safe environment for exploring the internal rules governing any situation.

Another common form of generalization is what linguists label as universal quantifiers. Words and phrases like *everyone, all, no one, never,* and *always* are often spoken as if the statement possesses a universal truth of which "everyone" is aware. By clarifying these terms, a supervisor helps the teacher ground the conversation with measurable details and supportable data. When the teacher says, "No one in my class completes their assignment," the supervisor might respond with a paraphrase and then inquire: "Your students are having some trouble getting their work done. Which of your students seem to be having the most difficulty finishing their work?"

The teacher reporting that her students are "very cooperative" may be a generalization. That would depend on how frequently and consistently she sees the behaviors she describes as cooperative. It is possible she is exhilarated by the success of one lesson. It is also possible that she has been monitoring performance in the critical attributes of cooperation for several weeks. Again, a thoughtful and well-framed inquiry clarifies and illuminates. A supervisor might ask, "As you think about the increase in cooperative behaviors, what percentage of the time would you say your students display these skills?" or "What percentage of your students have demonstrated marked improvement in their cooperative skills?"

Learning-Focused Supervision

Selecting Vague Terms for Clarification

It's important to recognize that not all vague terms need to be clarified. This is particularly true in learning-focused conversations. Skillful supervisors strategically choose terms that might be the most productive avenues to clarify the teacher's meaning. Without shared understanding, it is not possible for the supervisor to know what to explore. For example, when a teacher says, "My students are usually well-behaved," there's no way to know whether it's the entire class, what percentage of the time, or what would be examples of good behavior from the teacher's perspective. In the worst case, supervisors assume understanding without clarifying and respond from their own way of thinking. In the example above, a supervisor might impose their own definition of well-behaved, or assume that it's a large percentage of students, or that "usually" occurs more frequently than is true. There is potential for wasting valuable time if the conversation continues without clarification.

To develop the acuity for generating clarifying inquiries, supervisors listen for and inquire about percentage, frequency, duration, descriptors, examples, and under what contexts.

Table 4.2 Clarifying Vague Language

Listen/Inquire for	Teacher might say	Supervisor Strategy
Percentage (How many?)	*"I can't seem to get my students to listen carefully to one another during classroom discussions."*	*"Your students are not listening in the way you expect. What percentage of your students display this behavior?"*
Frequency (How often?)	*"I can't seem to get my students to listen carefully to one another during classroom discussions."*	*"So this issue concerns you. How often does this happen?"*
Duration (How long?)	*"I can't seem to get my students to listen carefully to one another during classroom discussions."*	*"You'd like more students to be more respectful of one another. How long has this been a concern?"*
Descriptors (Qualities)	*"I can't seem to get my students to listen carefully to one another during classroom discussions."*	*"You're finding that there is a lack of attention to others during classroom discussions. What are some indicators for when students listen carefully?"*
Examples (Which ones?)	*"I can't seem to get my students to listen carefully to one another during classroom discussions."*	*"You're noticing a lack of essential social skills. What are some examples of the listening behaviors that are most troubling?"*
Context (Under what conditions?)	*"I can't seem to get my students to listen carefully to one another during classroom discussions."*	*"You believe that your students should be attending fully to one another during classroom discussions. What are some conditions when they do or are more likely to listen to one another?"*

While each of these examples contain inquiries into vague language, some choices are likely to be more effective than others in producing clarity about the event or concern. For example, inquiring how long it takes the students to settle down is important information in aligning the supervisor's understanding with the teacher's expectations. Or asking about the number of students who are inattentive would help determine the scope of the problem. Increased clarity makes planning, reflecting, and problem-solving productive and growth promoting.

Implications & Applications: Clarifying Vague Language

Implications

Specificity in language encourages specificity in thinking and clarity in communication. Listening for and clarifying for vague language increases understanding and supports more effective planning, reflecting, and problem-solving.

1. What are some vague terms you use frequently in your own communication?

2. What are some vague terms you hear frequently from others (in person or in media)?

Applications

1. Spend fifteen minutes in a meeting or listening to media. Record the vague terms you hear.

2. Review samples of teacher lesson plans, school planning documents, and grade-level and department goals. Identify vague language and consider ways you might inquire to produce greater clarity.

Directing the Inquiry: The Topic

A mindful supervisor's choice of language for the topic of a question frames the scope of the response range. Potential topics span from higher to lower levels of abstraction. Inquiries with topics at higher levels of abstraction stimulate a broader range of responses. Inquiries with topics at lower levels of abstraction narrow the focus of the responses. For example, a question topic might be classroom management. Staying at a higher level of abstraction, the supervisor might ask, "What are some ways you monitor classroom management procedures?" The response categories might include instructional grouping, managing materials, or record keeping. Or lowering the level of abstraction, the topic could be narrowed to student transitions, "What are some ways you monitor student transitions?"

In this example, the responses might be directed towards maximizing instructional time, student clarity about what to do and where to move, or giving clear directions about expectations. Higher levels of abstraction include the names of teaching domains, in this case, 'Classroom Environment'. Lower levels of abstraction include indicators, critical attributes, or specific examples, such as inquiries about specific classroom routines, rules, or safety procedures.

Focusing the topic increases the time efficiency of the conversation by allowing the supervisor to move directly to critical areas while still inviting teacher thinking about the topic. Further, a more directed question feels safer for the teacher because there is less ambiguity about potential appropriate responses.

For example, at a broader level of inquiry, the supervisor might ask: "What are some of the learning environment qualities you hope to create in your classroom this year?" At a narrower level of inquiry, the supervisor might ask: "What are some essential routines you will need to establish at the start of the year?"

Learning-Focused Supervision

Developmental and Customized Inquiries

Teachers at different levels of practice are informed by distinct internal dialogues. Inquiries shape this self-talk. Aware supervisors assess current performance levels, envision the next level of practice, and craft questions to stimulate the kind of thinking that a more developmentally advanced teacher might apply. The intention is to motivate increasingly sophisticated awareness, interpretation, and ways of responding to classroom events. Ultimately, internalizing more expert ways of thinking reduces the cognitive load for growth-oriented practitioners.

Table 4.3 Developmental Inquiries

Present Practice	Desired Practice	Developmental Inquiry
Expected procedures are not practiced and reinforced, which leads to loss of instructional time	Management of routines, transitions, and classroom procedures is explicit and consistently applied	*"Given the importance of clear and consistent routines and procedures, what might be some indicators that your students have mastered or internalized expectations for things like transitions and material handling?"*
Lesson outcomes are not clearly communicated or assessed during and after instruction	Lesson outcomes are connected to the broader unit goals, communicated clearly, and assessed throughout the lesson	*"What are some ways you plan for and determine students' understanding of lesson outcomes and their connection to broader learning goals?"*
Responses from all students are encouraged, but only a few students are engaged. There's little discussion and students do not build on one another's ideas	Most students are involved in classroom discussions. The teacher applies a range of strategies to ensure greater inclusion and diversity of ideas	*"Your instructional design presumes a level of student skill for rich discussion and exchange of diverse ideas. What percentage of your students have those skills? What are some ways you might scaffold and develop the skills for those learners who are not there yet?"*

Increasing the Impact of Inquiries: Description to Thoughtfulness

Not all questions have equal value for promoting thinking and professional growth. An inquiry may contain all the elements and include an invitation, a cognitive focus, and a clear topic but still might elicit description rather than producing more complex levels of thought.

When a supervisor inquires for criteria for choice or success; sources of data, evidence, or information; or purposes or reasons, the teacher is guided to think deeply or more complexly.

Section 4: A Learning-Focused Tool Kit

Table 4.4 From Description to Thoughtfulness

Teacher says	Description question	Thoughtful inquiry
"I want my students to be respectful of each other, and I plan to do lots of collaborative work."	"What are some collaborative projects you are considering?"	Criteria: "As you think about your outcome of respect, what criteria might you use to determine your initial projects or to determine success?"
"I want my students to be respectful of each other, and I plan to do lots of collaborative work."	"What collaborative skills will your students need?"	Source of data: "Given that successful collaboration requires some fundamental skills, what are data sources you might use to determine student readiness?"
"I want my students to be respectful of each other, and I plan to do lots of collaborative work."	"What strategies will you use to develop collaborative skills?"	Purpose: "As you think about student collaboration, what are some things that are most important to you?"

Invitational Inquiry as a Habit

Well-crafted questions create opportunities for teachers to engage in thoughtful exchanges about professional practice. Questions that feel like interrogations shut down the necessary cognitive and emotional resources for these conversations. Effective supervisors consistently apply verbal and nonverbal routines that invite and encourage thoughtful responses. Automaticity with these skills frees the supervisor's emotional and cognitive energy to focus on the teacher's instructional thinking and development.

Developing Fluency with the Learning-Focused Tool Kit

The Learning-Focused Tool Kit is a vital resource for skillful communication with teachers as supervisors help them to plan, problem-solve, and reflect on practice. While the tools of attending fully, pausing, paraphrasing, and inquiring operate in concert with one another, they are easier to learn in isolation so each can be used automatically in a variety of settings. Purposeful practice of each tool individually leads to skills integration for fluent application within planning, reflecting, and problem-solving conversations and for fluid navigation of the Continuum of Learning-Focused Interaction.

Intentional learners transform skills into habits by isolating the component parts, overlearning the fundamentals, automatizing their use, and integrating these honed individual skills with the other tools in the tool kit.

The key to developing fluency with the Learning-Focused Tool Kit is to identify personal skill gaps and set small goals for isolated practice (see LFS Primary Traits Self-Assessment at **go.SolutionTree.com/leadership**).

TRANSFORMING SKILLS INTO HABITS
  isolate/
    overlearn/
      automatize/
        integrate

Figure 4.4 Invitational Inquiry Exercise Mat

INVITATIONAL INQUIRY

INVITATION	COGNITION	TOPIC
How might . . .	Predict	Outcomes
What would . . .	Recall	Curriculum
What are some . . .	Summarize	Instructional strategies
What might be some . . .	Identify	Student readiness
In what ways . . .	Describe	Student behavior
How might you . . .	Compare	Student work
What seem(s) . . .	Contrast	Student engagement
Given your . . .	Prioritize	Performance standards
Based on . . .	Interpret	Assessment results
Reflecting on . . .	Infer	Expectations
As you . . .	Conclude	Lesson
	Generalize	Materials
	Connect	Groups
	Apply	Classroom climate
	Evaluate	Procedures

EXAMPLES

What are some ways you are comparing this student's work to the performance standards?
(Invitation) (Cognition) (Topic)

Recalling your concerns, how might you address this student's behavior?
(Invitation) (Cognition) (Topic)

As you consider these assessment results what might be some priorities for next steps?
(Invitation) (Topic) (Invitation) (Cognition)

The Elements of the Invitation:
- Attending Fully
- Approachable Voice
- Plural Forms
- Exploratory Language
- Nondichotomous Forms
- Positive Presuppositions

Sample Stems:
- Given your knowledge of . . .
- Based on your experience with . . .
- Reflecting on . . .
- As you consider . . .

Syntactical Substitutions:
- the ― some
- could ― might
- is ― seems
- why ― what

SECTION 5

Data as a Tool for Growth

BEFORE YOU READ

1. Reflecting on your current practice, what are some ways you employ data in your supervisory conversations?
2. What are some of your experiences with ways teachers respond to data use in your supervisory conversations?

Observing and accurately assessing teaching performance is the foundation for meaningful conversations about a teacher's practice. Credible and accurate data are an indispensable resource for providing meaningful feedback to teachers during these conversations. However, without well-developed conferencing skills, all the time and effort put into data collection has little value and little influence on teacher thinking, decision-making, and behavioral change. Emerging studies bear out the need for investing in supervisors' abilities to shape learning-focused conversations with teachers in their schools (Sartain et al., 2011). These conversations are most meaningful and effective when grounded in clear, low-inference, and relevant data. Such data illuminate standards by transforming abstract descriptions into contextually vivid images of a teacher's practice.

Data and Standards

As noted in Section One, standards only become useful professional guidelines when they can be objectively measured, and when practitioners have shared understandings of the meanings of the metrics. Data-based assessments organized by scales and rubrics then become the focal point of growth-promoting conversations between teachers and supervisors. Comparing teaching performance to standards (as opposed to comparing teachers to one another) increases the objectivity of both the data collection and any judgments related to those data. The skilled use of standards-based observation processes, including both data collection and thoughtfully delivered feedback, is strongly related to student achievement gains (Carter & Welner, 2013).

No professional is at the top of the scale in all performance arenas. Data-based assessments organized by scales and rubrics produce fine-grained scores that clarify the subsets of an overall rating for a given teaching standard. For example, not all ratings of 3 are the same. Data illuminates the distinctions between the various elements and components of a given standard in order to identify both accomplishments and target areas for growth. For example, two teachers might each receive the same overall rating for their ability to communicate with students; one of these teachers has a higher rating for her skills in giving directions and the other has greater skills with explaining concepts and sharing content information. By clarifying the rationale for these subscores, the supervisor is then able to work with each teacher to set meaningful professional learning goals. Skilled supervisors are mindful of avoiding personal bias, establishing relevancy, and reducing overload when selecting, collecting, and sharing data.

Learning-Focused Supervision

Avoiding Bias: The Importance of Low-Inference Data

Trust in the process is a vital component for maintaining the integrity and effectiveness of any supervisory relationship. To trust the process, teachers need to trust the data. All data are not created equal. Objectivity is the foundation of an effective performance appraisal. Therefore, the most valuable data are specific, concrete, and low-inference—focused on what is seen and heard without assumptions or judgments. These data allow for the objective examination of facts, without biases, based on what is actually going on in the classroom. Note the following examples.

> **Low-inference:** Five of eighteen students finished their "Do It Now" and were off-task for the remainder of the allotted time, waiting for next-step instructions.
>
> **High-inference:** The lesson pacing was too slow.
>
> **Low-inference:** At the start of the period, the teacher asked preassigned homework partners to review each other's work and then randomly selected students (drawing popsicle-stick name markers to select students) to come to the board and explain how they arrived at their answers.
>
> **High-inference:** The teacher put students in pairs to keep them engaged and on-task while reviewing homework.

"To trust the process, teachers need to trust the data."

To reduce—and ideally eliminate—bias, supervisors need to be self-aware and disciplined with collecting, examining, and analyzing data. Unconscious bias is often based on the supervisor's initial impressions or perceptions of others. A bias rating error is any attitude or tendency on the part of the supervisor to respond in a way that impedes objectivity and accuracy in the evaluation process. These biases include the following errors.

First-Impression Error

This error bias is the tendency of a rater to make an initial judgment, whether positive or negative, and then distort subsequent information to support the initial judgment.

For example: Mr. G's desk is neat, and his materials stations are well-organized, so the supervisor assumes a well-managed classroom. Conversely, Ms. J's classroom displays are out of date and off-kilter, which causes the supervisor to look for other examples of sloppy performance.

Recency or Spillover Error

This error bias is related to First-Impression Error in that the rater tends to assess based on the most recent performance, then rates subsequent performances consistent with that previous rating. Or the supervisor makes an assessment based on previous history without taking changes—decline or improvement in performance—into account.

For example: Ms. L is consistently argumentative during staff meetings, so the supervisor is more likely to look for negative examples during her classroom observation.

Halo (or Horns) Error

In this error bias, performance is rated based on a supervisor's perception of a teacher—whether overly positive or negative—that influences the entire appraisal, or it causes the supervisor to form generalizations based on one aspect of practice.

For example: Mr. W needs to repeat directions and loses instructional time. After observing this behavior, the supervisor tends to see other negative examples of performance.

Just-Like-Me Error

This error bias causes the supervisor to evaluate more favorably those practitioners who they perceive as similar to themselves.

For example: Ms. Q's classroom echoes the supervisor's own room when he was teaching. Thus the supervisor is more likely to look for positive examples during an observation.

Central-Bias or Negative/Positive Error

This error bias is the tendency of a supervisor to score teachers at the extreme ends of the scale, too harshly or too leniently, or close to the midpoint of a scale when their performance justifies a substantially lower or higher rating.

For example: The supervisor never gives more than a 2 on anything or always gives 3's to everyone.

Emotional-State Error

This error bias is the tendency of a supervisor to allow their present emotional state or present relationship with the teacher influence the rating.

For example: The supervisor had a difficult conversation with a parent before a classroom visit, and the resulting annoyance puts a negative lens on the observation.

Strategies for Avoiding Bias

All performance ratings should be established based on clear standards and low-inference data and not be compared to previous performance, initial impressions, personal relationship, or any other factors other than observable evidence aligned with a rubric. Some ways to avoid bias errors include careful analysis of ratings to ensure the data aligns with the rubric, especially in circumstances where there is previous history—positive or negative—with a colleague; being skeptical if a teacher's scores indicate "exceeds expectations" or "needs improvement" on every component; taking caution when reviewing the data if there has been a recent exchange or experience with a teacher which has been particularly positive or negative.

Learning-Focused Supervision

Choosing Data to Ensure Relevancy

Choosing data means choosing perspective. Relevant data are based on standards, teacher goals, or grade-level, school, and district priorities. Thus both teacher performance and student-learning data would be included. An important intention for a learning-focused conversation is to make explicit the cause/effect relationship between teacher actions and student outcomes.

Performance data for teachers can include observation scripts and video logs, as well as artifacts such as lesson plans, student work products, and parent communications. An environmental scan provides data on the physical set-up of the classroom including furniture arrangements, student access to materials, and the ways in which classroom displays support and reflect student learning.

Student data includes summative assessment results as well as formative tools such as student work samples, videos of classroom interactions, student surveys, journals and learning logs, running records, checklists, and report card grades. Supervisor scripts and classroom videos can provide information about elements such as students' level of engagement, time on task, and ability to follow directions.

Determining and agreeing upon the data-focus is an important consideration for customizing learning-focused supervision. For example, if a teacher's goal is to increase student participation, data sources might include video clips capturing which students are engaged and what they are saying and doing, response checklists, observations of teacher wait time and discourse patterns.

These data are vehicles for investigating the teacher's effectiveness of quantity and quality of student participation.

Avoiding Overload: Sharing the Data

Effective use of data supports a developmental approach to learning-focused supervision. Thoughtful supervisors consider the learning needs of individual teachers by prioritizing which data are collected, how they are organized, and how they are shared.

Effective supervisors attend to these choices when choosing data during planning, when analyzing data to prepare for reflection, and while reflecting with the teacher.

Cognitive Load Theory

Cognitive Load Theory (CLT) (Sweller, 1988) offers an explanatory framework for how the brain processes and stores information. Humans have two forms of memory: working memory and long-term memory. Working memory is used for processing new information. That mental activity produces a "cognitive load" which affects learning outcomes. When information is successfully integrated into new or existing mental schemas it moves into long-term memory for storage and later retrieval. When too much new information is presented to learners' working memories, their brains get overloaded and learning shuts down.

Overwhelming teachers with too much or difficult-to-decipher data can produce an unmanageable cognitive load that limits the ability to take in, make sense of, or be able to act on the information provided.

Section 5: Data as a Tool for Growth

EXPERT MOVE
Skilled supervisors avoid cognitively and emotionally overloading teachers with too much data when providing performance feedback. They are careful to match the amount and type of data to the developmental needs of their teachers.

Applying Data in Learning-Focused Conversations

Data have no meaning. Raw numbers, scores, and scales are simply information without significance until these measurements are organized, analyzed, and interpreted. Frames of reference—ways of seeing the world—become lenses through which we create meaning from the collected data. Standards-based, learning-focused conversations shape these lenses and promote shared understanding between teachers and supervisors about teaching and learning purposes and processes (see Section 3: Structured Conversations).

Data are a vital resource for driving productive planning, reflecting, and problem-solving conversations.

In planning conversations, data are essential for defining student learning outcomes and issues that need to be addressed and demonstrating success and goal achievement. These indicators will, in many cases, be for both short- and long-term desired outcomes.

In reflecting conversations, data analysis links evidence to impressions and judgments. The data collected, for example in the form of teacher and supervisor observations and exploration of student work samples, grounds the conversation in the search for patterns and provides a source for comparing desired goals with results and for contrasting the work of successful students with those who have not yet met identified learning targets. Data-focused cause/effect analysis allows teachers and supervisors to dig deeply into the factors influencing student learning results.

In problem-solving conversations, data help to define both the scope of the concern and degree of importance for addressing this issue. As in the planning conversation, data are essential for defining indicators of success that will measure any envisioned outcomes for meeting this challenge.

Using Data in Each Stance of the Continuum of Learning-Focused Interaction

In the Continuum of Learning-Focused Interaction, data amplifies the potency of each stance.

Data are the foundation for inquiry in the coaching stance and increase the learning potential of that stance. Similarly, in the collaborative stance, data are the gateway to the pursuit of ideas, possibilities, and perspectives. In the consulting stance, data provide the basis for suggestions and choices. And when calibrating, the supervisor uses data to align judgment with the standards and substantiate claims and directives.

Data are essential in all the stances in order to increase contextual relevancy by making any comment, suggestion, or collaboration specific to the teacher's classroom.

Learning-Focused Supervision

Table 5.1 Using Data with The Continuum of Learning-Focused Interaction

Stance	Example
When Calibrating	"These data indicate that 35% of your students have mastered the objective on word usage. The expectation for third grade is 80% or above. You will need to develop strategies for improving student success with these reading skills."
When Consulting	"Given the data on student vocabulary, there are several potential strategies that might address improvement: incorporating daily word games to liven interest and knowledge, pre-teaching the academic vocabulary needed for content area reading, and perhaps more read-alouds and use of multimedia to build background knowledge."
When Collaborating	"The data indicate a gap in student performance on this objective. Let's generate some factors that might be causing this deficit."
When Coaching	"These data display a clear deficit for some students in vocabulary development. What's your sense of the skills that students have who are mastering this objective as opposed to students who aren't?"
Stance to Data	**Example**
Calibrating with Data	"It's important for all students to stay engaged during math instruction and you'll need to implement strategies towards that end. These data indicate that 8 of your 22 learners were off-task during this lesson."
Consulting with Data	"There are several strategies you might try in order to increase student attention, engagement, and responsibility: make smaller groups and try shifting from groups of four to partners; try formative assessments like using random selection for responding to questions or showing work on the board; or create a reward system graphing individual achievement and rewarding students who continually best their best scores. Implementing one or more of these ideas is critical, because the data are clear that students are zoning out during math instruction."
Collaborating with Data	"Let's generate some ideas for increasing student engagement, specifically applied to math instruction. These observational data indicate there was a lack of engagement for almost 30% of your students."
Coaching with Data	"What's your sense of how these data reflect students' involvement in areas other than math, given that these data show that during math instruction, there was a lack of engagement and attention for about a third of your students?"

Data as a Third Point

Using data as a third point (see Applying the Third Point, p. 31) is especially important for maintaining psychological safety for a teacher. Data become a mirror reflecting both the positive aspects of teaching choices and results as well as any attributes the supervisor or teacher might find less effective. Using a third point depersonalizes the materials under consideration by shifting the focus from the teacher-supervisor relationship to the data they are reviewing. This process allows both parties to address the information as objective evidence. Establishing data as a third point is especially important when supervisors conduct formative and summative conferences that are part of teacher evaluation procedures.

Section 5: Data as a Tool for Growth

Getting Started with Data

Exploring data during learning-focused interactions is the key to effective examination and improvement of teaching and learning outcomes. Yet data often create discomfort or even anxiety for practitioners. The high-pressure push for continuous progress has made data seem more threatening than productive when the purpose is to prove rather than improve. Skilled supervisors share clear intentions and create a safe space for investigation when they place data in the center of learning-focused conversations. In concert with the skillful use of nonjudgmental listening and invitational language, these data-driven discussions lead to thoughtful discovery, context-based assessments, and the identification of developmentally appropriate goals.

EXPERT MOVE

Skillful supervisors study success with their teachers by providing data that reveal effective results. This emphasis on what is working versus what is not working increases teacher confidence and enhances psychological safety. This pattern provides a rich opportunity to explore causality and encourages the transfer of successful teaching behaviors to new situations.

"Skilled supervisors share clear intentions and create a safe space for investigation when they place data in the center of learning-focused conversations."

Types of Data

A critical part of learning-focused supervision is determining how much and which sources of data will best serve a conversation. Learning-focused conversations can draw from two distinctly different types of data: qualitative and quantitative. Qualitative data tend to be descriptive and holistic and include such things as portfolios, surveys, checklists, and diagrams. Quantitative data are numbers-based and include formative and summative test scores, percentages, amounts, and tallies. For example, qualitative observational data might include a verbatim account of what students say in response to a teacher's question, while the quantitative correlate might be the number or percentage of students who responded.

In addition to data type, the perspective, time frame, and scope are also key variables. That is, data can be collected about teacher behaviors or student behaviors: the most recently observed information or observations over time and focused on a particular student or group of students or based on a full class or several classes (see Table 5.2 Examples of Quantitative and Qualitative Data).

EXPERT MOVE

Skilled supervisors thoughtfully identify, collect, and display data that's matched to teacher learning goals. Such data are a tactical mix of the many forms of information about teacher behaviors and student responses.

Table 5.2 Examples of Quantitative and Qualitative Data

	Quantitative (how many, how much)	Qualitative (Looks like, sounds like)
Teacher	• Number of stopping points to redirect student behavior within class period • Percentage of instructional time disrupted or lost during a lesson, week, or marking period • Number of teacher questions • Length of wait time offered to students • Teacher – student talk ratios • Time markers to measure lesson pace • Frequency/duration of time spent in full class/small groups • Chart reflecting number of times students are called on • Number of opportunities for student responses – peer-to-peer – and students to teacher	• Brief videos with specific focus (e.g., giving directions, creating closure) • Verbatim scripts (e.g., teacher directions, inquiries, responses to students' questions) • Diagrams (e.g., movement around the classroom, room set-up, response patterns) • Photos (e.g., classroom displays, room arrangement, activity centers) • Samples of formative assessments, homework assignments, correspondence with parents • Descriptions/types of disciplinary interventions • Lesson/unit plans
Student	• Formal assessment results • Student Reading/Math assessment scores • Classroom records (e.g., attendance rates, percent of assignment completion, behavioral incidents) • Percentage of students on-task/off-task • Length of time for transitions • Number of student questions • Number of students volunteering answers • Number of students responding to or extending peer responses	• Report cards • Student portfolios • Student work products • Rubrics/Scales/Checklists • Descriptions of on-task/off-task behaviors • Lists of which students initiate questions/ideas/problem solutions • Diagrams/descriptions of student interaction patterns - who is working with whom and in what ways • Script of student responses - to teacher and to each other

Data provide a focus for analyzing practice and instructional outcomes. Connecting and cross-referencing multiple types of data, or triangulating, results in a comprehensive picture of teacher performance. For example, making connections between a verbatim script of teacher questions, the length and frequency of wait time, and a script of student responses provides a rich examination of classroom discourse. Or comparing the frequency of on/off task behavior, a script of teacher directions, and related lesson plans might energize a conversation about ways to keep students engaged. Assessing performance based on insufficient data limits the opportunity to stimulate learning and growth.

Section 5: Data as a Tool for Growth

Video as a Data Source

Video of classroom interactions is an underutilized source of low-inference data. Videos recorded on readily accessible smartphone and tablet cameras offer a view of teaching practices and learner experiences that are often difficult to collect through other means. Video captures teacher behaviors and student responses that might otherwise go unnoticed. This lens offers objective details which allows teachers and supervisors to explore and analyze classroom dynamics and outcomes.

Clarifying the focus of a video is an essential element of any planning conversation. The intention of the video should be to collect data that will illuminate the goals being pursued during the lesson.

During reflecting conversations, the videos become engaging third points. With these data available, a skillful supervisor navigates the continuum, starting from a coaching stance and shifting stances depending on what the teacher sees and hears. The ability to replay sections of lessons allows supervisors and teachers to home in on specific moments and clarify the specifics to interpret events and construct meaning.

As with any data, it is important to share the video with the teacher prior to meeting to allow time for thoughtful review.

Using Data in Structured Conversations

Clarifying Goals: The Planning Conversation

A planning conversation is a guided design experience that draws on data in multiple ways. First, it illuminates the current state of classroom conditions and student performance levels and then clarifies the types of data that will measure progress in achieving appropriate next level goals.

For example, data are drawn upon to respond to the first few questions in the planning template: a search for details about classroom dynamics and current needs and expectations for students. Types of data for this purpose might include assessment scores, attendance records, student work products, and other descriptive and numbers-based sources.

One important function of a planning conversation is to make goals visible. Ultimately, the goal must be expressed in ways that are observable and measurable. During the planning conversation, supervisors and teachers identify and agree upon data that would support assessment of whether and to what degree outcomes are being achieved.

Supervisor might ask:	Teacher might respond:
"What are some ways your assessment scores influence your math lesson design?"	*"I can see that about 35% of my kids have the foundation for the next concept, but I'm concerned about the rest. I need to consider reviews, or scaffolds, or some combination of both."*
"So you have some ideas for the kids that are not quite there. What are some thoughts about the students who are ready for next steps?"	*"I'd like to create a short assessment that includes some items that confirm understanding of the current outcomes and next-level outcomes."*

Learning-Focused Supervision

Feedback Loops

Feedback loops are an essential organizing feature of biological and human-made systems. Feedback occurs when some portion of a system's output cycles back to influence future behavior.

A thermostat is a classic example of a feedback loop. Setting the desired temperature tells the system to maintain itself to this specification. Air or water flows in the heating or cooling system as the thermostat reads the "data" and either continues further flow or pauses the system when it senses goal achievement.

In human learning situations, timely and thoughtful feedback, in which desired goals are compared to current outcomes, forms a feedback loop that determines success and clarifies performance gaps. When supervisors collect data about student and teacher performances, organize and frame the data during learning-focused conversations, and engage teachers in meaning-making processes, productive feedback loops are established. These loops link teacher perceptions, decisions, and actions to student learning products and performances. When teachers and supervisors identify gaps between desired outcomes and present results, they then cycle back to the originating decisions that drove the instructional choices and form the basis for both next-step thinking and for reconsidering the basic lesson design or modifying a specific classroom practice.

Data and Inquiries: The Reflecting Conversation

A reflecting conversation is a guided learning experience that is also data-driven. Initially, anecdotal recollection is used to surface successes and areas of concern. These qualitative data sources reveal what stands out most for the teacher. At this point, data might be referenced (from either the supervisor or the teacher) to further investigate these impressions.

Data-driven exploration is the driving force of these conversations. Reviewing the data stimulates thinking about what occurred and why. Ultimately, these data explorations support the framing of generalizations about the takeaways from the lesson and envisioning targeted applications for future lessons and refinements in teaching practices.

Supervisor might ask:	Teacher might respond:
"As you consider these charts of student participation, what are some patterns you notice?"	"A few things stand out that surprise me. I see that there was lots of participation, but mostly from the students in front. And also, more kids responded at the beginning of the lesson than at the end."
"So there are two things you notice: participation related to both seating arrangement and sequence of instruction. What's your hunch about what might be producing those results?"	"Well, the beginning of the lesson is review, so it makes sense that more students were able to respond. As the lesson progressed, the questions were more challenging. And of course, my higher-performing kids tend to sit up front, so that might account for that result."

Reflecting with Data
vimeo.com/miravia/
reflecting-with-data

OR

Section 5: Data as a Tool for Growth

Supervisor might ask:	Teacher might respond:
"Given the recollections you've just described, what are some examples of student work that support your impressions?"	"Here are four writing samples where kids supported their claims with evidence from the text—which was what they were expected to do—that are representative of what about 80% of the class achieved."
"Seems like it was an effective lesson. What's your hunch about what is producing such successful writers?"	"One thing I've changed is that I'm much more explicit about teaching how to craft an argument, and I do more modeling of each element. And I make sure to check for understanding before moving on."

EXPERT MOVE

Skillful supervisors recognize and prepare for dissonance and disagreement. They are careful to gather and display low-inference data as a third point for the conversation.

Searching for Solution: The Problem-Solving Conversation

A problem-solving conversation applies data to problem framing and solution generation. Initially, data are used to define the parameters of an issue or concern, to identify and monitor success indicators, and then to guide the development of potential causal theories. A clear problem definition creates a platform for identifying the data that will measure progress and define success. With these two elements in place, a supervisor and teacher can then tap data to generate and test causal theories before launching a plan for solution.

Targeted data use defines the parameters of an issue or concern. Data can help clarify the magnitude, scope, and degree of importance of any given issue, which may reduce the emotional load. Clarifying progress indicators increases teacher efficacy for staying the course with solution efforts.

Supervisor might ask:	Teacher might respond:
"Given your concerns about students being responsible with lab equipment, what percentage of your students have not yet mastered the appropriate protocols?"	"Based on my observations, I would say it's easily 75% in each of my lab periods."
"So it seems to be a fairly big problem. As you consider their behavior, what would you look and listen for to track their development of the necessary lab skills?"	"One idea would be to use a checklist to determine which skills each student has mastered and monitor progress in that way."

Learning-Focused Supervision

Data-Based Discoveries During Learning-Focused Conversations

In productive and time-efficient learning-focused conversations, supervisors and teachers use data to make connections between teaching choices and learning results. The data serve as a foundation for consulting, collaborating, and coaching as skillful supervisors guide exchanges that produce new understandings by highlighting the relationship between student learning data and teacher performance data (see Table 5.1 Using Data with the Continuum of Learning-Focused Interaction).

For example, during a planning conversation, some predictions might be made between the teacher's pacing and student engagement or how strategies for distributed responses would produce increased active participation. Or a reflecting conversation might illuminate the relationship between wait time and the amount of student participation or between a teacher's level of questioning and student thoughtfulness. In a problem-solving conversation, connections between the teacher's movement patterns in the classroom might help define some issues around student attention or on-task behavior.

Drawing upon multiple types of data from differing perspectives for teacher actions and student behaviors enriches learning-focused conversations and enhances the opportunity to learn from such exchanges. This is especially true when skilled supervisors prepare for a conversation by analyzing and annotating the data. For example, sorting by standard elements and components or scripting teacher's questions and tallying the number of student responses for each reveals patterns, frequencies, and percentages of various measures that can be highlighted and explored.

> **EXPERT MOVE**
>
> Skillful supervisors send annotated data to teachers ahead of time so there is an opportunity for thoughtful review in preparation for a face-to-face conversation.

Four Qualities of Learning-Focused Supervision in Action

Improving teacher skills at all levels of development draws on the four qualities of learning-focused supervision described in Section One. Data-based practices intertwine with the other three qualities to support growth along the pathways leading to increasing instructional expertise.

Data use is customized in a variety of ways, including identifying performance aspects related to teaching and learning standards that will focus the data collection, the variety and types of data that will be collected to assess these targets, and the selection of which of these data will be shared with the teacher.

Data use is developmental when supervisors and teachers define learning targets and achievable increments of growth for the teacher and the students. The data collected can then be used to measure progress, refine goals, and support a vision of continuous learning and high expectations for the teacher and the students.

Data use is standards-driven when supervisors and teachers reference and articulate appropriate teaching and learning criteria as they plan, reflect, and problem-solve. The data help to clarify a given standard and are used to define performance gaps and gains and establish targeted learning goals for students and teachers.

The melding of these four qualities establishes a learning rich environment that energizes the working relationship between supervisors and teachers.

Implications & Applications: Using Data

Implications

Skillful data use is a catalyst for teacher learning and growth. Identifying and analyzing a variety of data sources offers perspectives for examining teaching and learning practices.

1. What are some of the data types you typically use in your supervisory work with teachers?
2. What are some of the factors that contribute to the effective use of data during your supervisory conversations?

Applications

1. Review Table 5.2 Examples of Quantitative and Qualitative Data and select several types that you do not typically use and try them out in upcoming conversations.
2. For your upcoming supervisory conversations, review your observational notes and annotations, identify any inferences, and edit to provide supporting evidence.
3. Practice using data as a third point to focus your conversations.

Learning-Focused Supervision

Notes · Insights · Applications

SECTION 6

From Novice to Expert Teaching

BEFORE YOU READ

1. What are some of the differences that you notice between the classroom practices of novice teachers and those of more expert teachers?

2. What are some ways that you modify your supervisory practices to address the learning needs of teachers across a range of instructional skills?

To the casual eye, expert teaching appears to be a rare form of alchemy that blends content knowledge, instructional skills, and the ability to connect with students, all combined with a splash of charisma to catalyze the mix. But we now know that expert teaching is an acquired and ever-expanding body of knowledge and skills that are available to anyone open to learning from their classroom experiences. Developing from novice to more expert teacher is one of the most daunting professional journeys in our society. This quest is a lifetime's work for practitioners who are committed to growing and improving throughout their career.

The adult learning environment in a school can either sustain or inhibit teacher growth and development. Skillful supervision is an essential part of a support system that encourages essential trial and error during the learning processes through which teaching skills develop. Supervisors who establish a safe environment for risk-taking help teachers stretch beyond their comfort zones so they can continually expand their professional know-how and expertise. Given the ever-shifting conditions inside and outside schools, being a learning-focused teacher and a learning-focused supervisor are essential dispositions for long-term career success.

Mindful supervisors strategically choose specific circuits to stimulate and reinforce in individual teachers. Careful observation and analysis of classroom practices and products referenced to teaching and learning standards offers insights into which teacher brain circuits are robust and efficient and which need additional stimulation. The templates for planning, reflecting, and problem-solving found in Section Three illustrate the fundamental thinking circuits that drive effective instructional design and delivery.

Two Types of Expertise: Routine and Adaptive

Expertise appears in two forms: routine expertise and adaptive expertise (Hatano & Inagaki, 1986). Routine expertise is the most readily observed form. This is the expertise of the artisan who can efficiently and consistently

Expertise and the Brain: Practice Matters

Just as teachers in their classrooms are responsible for developing the steadily maturing brains of students, supervisors too are in the brain-growing business. Expert teachers think and respond differently than novice teachers. It's not only the differences in experience, but also physical differences in brain structures and circuitry. As in any field or craft, improving teaching skills requires changes in the cognitive architecture of the learner. All human thoughts, emotions, and control of physical actions flow across the brain as precisely timed electrical signals traveling through chains of neurons to form neural networks linked to the original stimulus. A white fatty substance called myelin sheathes bundles of nerve fibers as they develop. Like insulation on the wiring of a house, the protective myelin coating increases the speed, strength, and accuracy of the electrical impulses in the brain. Repeated firings of a neural circuit stimulate additional myelin production. These new layers increase the fluency and robustness of thoughts and movements (Coyle, 2009).

Learning-Focused Supervision

produce high-quality products and performances according to tested recipes. Experienced bakers craft trays of breads, pies, and pastries daily that are pleasing to the eye and taste buds. Muscle memory for mixing and kneading the various doughs is automatic and allows the baker to flow from counter to pan to the oven and back with seemingly little mental energy.

Master bakers who are more adaptive experts can invent fresh recipes by combining ingredients in innovative and sometimes unconventional ways. Their conceptual knowledge of the chemistry and physics of flavors and textures permits them to see new possibilities and create new forms. This adaptive mindset rests on a foundation of routine expertise, but adaptive capacities do not automatically emerge from fundamental craft knowledge and competence. Adaptive reasoning develops through test cases and experimentation, reflecting on experiences, and feedback from knowledgeable colleagues.

Expert teaching requires a full complement of both routine and adaptive expertise. Necessary classroom skills such as getting attention, giving directions, calling on students, and other essentials of classroom management all require routine expertise. Internalizing basic instructional moves can free a teacher's mental and emotional energy for the deeper work of orchestrating classroom dynamics for rich content and cognitively stimulating learning. Mastery of these requisite teaching skills develops through deliberate practice with guidance from mentors, coaches, and supervisors.

Adaptive Expertise in Teaching

High levels of teaching performance require additional levels of adeptness or adaptive expertise. This degree of skill requires the ability to apply knowledge to novel problems, especially those that are atypical cases within

---

Deliberate Practice

All physical and mental skills are organized into chunks in the brain. These mental networks, once developed through practice and repetition, are held in long-term memory. Each chunk has distinctive elements and features that are biochemically coded for ease of retrieval. Experts have many more available chunks than novices. Their more robustly developed mental representations and automaticity with essential skills allow them to manage greater complexity while conserving cognitive and emotional energy when performing instructional actions.

When these units are fully integrated in the brain's mental circuitry, humans develop skill automaticity that is often outside of conscious awareness. This muscle memory provides the ease of execution that is admired in the masters of any craft or art form. Successful coaches and instructors in all fields—from sports to music and medicine and more—help their learners break down the chunks into three levels: 1) the master illuminates the big chunk or mega-circuit that holds the task or skill as a whole; 2) the master breaks down tasks or skills into the smallest possible segments that can be practiced as units; 3) the master regulates performance time by slowing actions down for conscious skill development, then bringing it up to speed for skill execution. In this way the coach or instructor helps the learner develop the inner architecture of the desired skill or skill cluster (Coyle, 2009). For example, when teachers call a class to attention, they draw on physical skills for body placement in the teaching space, postural and tonal awareness to establish credibility, and verbal facility to convey the importance of the messages (Grinder, 1997). Many beginning teachers and struggling veteran teachers have difficulty with this fundamental instructional task and lose valuable learning time when they need to focus student energy and alertness.

a given domain, such as a specific content topic or student developmental level. This form of adaptive expertise means that practitioners can determine the important features of a problem and invent new procedures that move beyond any existing repertoire. For teachers, this might mean addressing student misconceptions, crafting enriching and stimulating curriculum, or supporting students with developing their own complex reasoning skills within specific content areas.

Adaptive experts refine their knowledge and skills by reflecting on and learning from their experiences, especially when things don't turn out as planned. Learning-focused supervisors mediate this type of expertise by inquiring into the possible sources of unexpected outcomes. They engage teachers in exploring why these results might have occurred and generating potential alternatives for future practice. Applying this approach with teachers at all developmental levels is an important resource for expanding the learning culture in schools.

Five Spheres of Teaching Expertise

The growing knowledge base about teaching is a rich resource for promoting professional growth for teachers at all stages of their career (Saphier, Haley-Speca & Gower, 2018). The ways that practitioners mentally organize knowledge and apply it to the learning processes in their classrooms frames both instructional design and delivery as well as personal approaches to problem-solving.

The knowledge of teaching expertise can be organized into five spheres: 1) knowledge of the structure of the discipline(s); 2) knowledge of teaching skills and strategies; 3) knowledge of learners and learning; 4) knowledge of self; and 5) knowledge of collaboration (see Figure 6.1 Five Spheres of Teaching Expertise). These spheres offer frameworks for exploring growth areas for teachers at all developmental levels. They provide a way for supervisors to structure learning-focused conversations with teachers, to set professional learning goals, and to gather resources for supporting and sustaining growth in craft knowledge and skills. The five spheres are also useful diagnostic lenses for analyzing issues that might arise when a teacher has persistent difficulties. By searching for deeper developmental gaps, the supervisor can then plan appropriate interventions that target certain areas for growth.

Figure 6.1 Five Spheres of Teaching Expertise

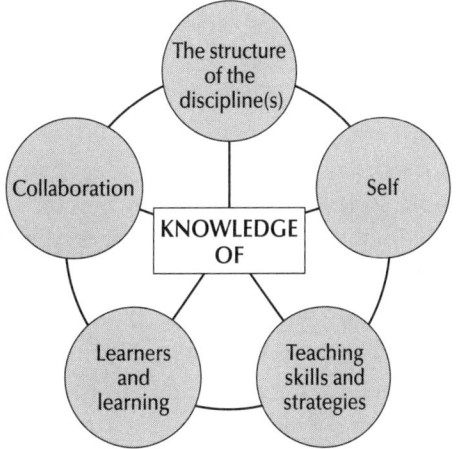

Knowledge of the Structure of the Discipline

Teacher knowledge of the structure of a given content discipline correlates highly with student success in that domain. Knowledge alone is insufficient. Expert teachers also understand the organization of knowledge within each content area and within specific topics. Knowing the structure of the discipline means knowing the big ideas within a content area, including the organizing principles, key concepts, and the ways in which these influence one another (Wiggins & McTighe, 2005; Shulman, 1987). Curricular frameworks as presented in national, state, and provincial standards delineate essential outcomes and serve as important references for supervisor-teacher conversations.

The greater the depth of a teacher's content understanding, the greater their ability to design and customize learning units. This level of knowledge increases instructional flexibility and the likelihood that students can develop their own meaningful cognitive maps (Darling-Hammond & Bransford, 2005). When a teacher's understanding is fragmented, it contributes to student misconceptions within a content area. In elementary mathematics, for example, understanding means being able to explain and illustrate a sense of number and how various operations such as addition and subtraction relate to each other. In social studies, it means showing students how to apply geographic, political, historical, economic, and social perspectives to a given situation.

Real learning is messy. Teachers with rich structural knowledge are more flexible and resourceful with meeting the challenges that arise during classroom lessons. Students do not always fit neatly within the boundaries of lesson plans. Therefore, teacher content knowledge must always be greater and more fully integrated than that of their students. This level of understanding allows teachers to prioritize and select the most appropriate content objectives for students.

During planning, reflecting, and problem-solving conversations, effective supervisors listen carefully for gaps in a teacher's understanding of important curricular ideas. Creating a climate in which it is safe for a teacher to ask for help with content knowledge is a necessary condition for growth. No one knows everything about any discipline. This is especially true for elementary teachers and secondary teachers who are assigned to more than one content area. Providing resource materials and including mini tutorials during conversations reduces anxiety, and at the same time it helps to ensure content accuracy for that teacher's students. This is especially important when working with beginning teachers and with experienced teachers who are teaching a course or topic for the first time.

At times, it is useful for both novice and more experienced supervisors to consult with content specialists, such as department chairs, curriculum coordinators, and skilled instructional coaches, when they have questions or concerns about the accuracy of a teacher's content delivery. Experts can help clarify gaps and misunderstandings of critical concepts and provide resources for the supervisor to share with teachers.

It is essential that teachers understand and are able to model the specialized ways of thinking in a given field. Literature and physical science, for example, each have their own principles of inquiry. In social studies, ideas are organized in specific ways. Mathematics has a rich problem-solving repertoire. Writing narrative text is different than writing expository text. Each of these ways of knowing is an important element within a content area. By promoting these skills and perspectives, teachers help students discover how those who produce knowledge and knowing in a specific domain develop and modify ideas. So, too, supervisors create these understandings for their teachers during learning-focused conversations.

Each content area includes a minefield of misconceptions. Experienced teachers learn to anticipate these as they appear within curriculum topics. Lesson plans reflect this thinking as teachers design ways to surface and dispel barriers to deeper understanding. Knowing which misconceptions are developmentally appropriate at certain stages of learning is valuable craft knowledge. Knowing how to help students work through them is even more useful.

Knowledge of the structure of a discipline is specific to each content area. For example, at the elementary level, this knowledge informs the approach to instruction in mathematics or reading (Hill, Rowan & Ball, 2005; Snow, Griffin & Burns, 2005). For secondary teachers, this knowledge usually means specific topics within a curriculum.

For example, one study of first-year biology teachers noted that when novices presented topics about which they had great depth of knowledge, they let their classes explore ideas as they asked open-ended questions and promoted richer classroom discourse. When novices were less confident in their own content knowledge, their lessons were structured more rigidly, they talked more than their students, and they asked lower cognitive level questions (Carlson, 1993).

A teacher's approach to a subject area is a special consideration for supervisors of both elementary and secondary teachers. A teacher's degree of knowledge in a given content area or curriculum topic may influence their choice of stance or percentage of time spent in a particular stance—calibrating, consulting, collaborating, or coaching—during a learning-focused conversation. While all teachers encounter a general set of universal challenges, it's useful to analyze content-specific issues for possible interventions. For example, if classroom management issues crop up at specific times of day, a teacher's comfort with a subject area may be a factor to consider.

> "Creating a climate in which it is safe for a teacher to ask for help with content knowledge is a necessary condition for growth. No one knows everything about any discipline."

Implications & Applications: Knowledge of the Structure of the Discipline

Implications

Teachers' rich structural knowledge of their disciplines is the foundation for developing effective units and lessons and supports instructional flexibility when interacting with students.

1. What are some of your strengths when supporting teachers with specific content areas?
2. What are some of your stretch areas when supporting teachers with specific content areas?

Applications

1. When working with high-performing teachers, note the examples and models they use to illustrate the content and concepts of their discipline. During reflecting conversations with these more expert teachers, reference these examples and models and explore the ways that these help students develop the deeper understandings within the curriculum. Note these examples for use when consulting with less knowledgeable teachers.
2. Develop a network of content specialists to support you and your teachers, especially for curriculum areas that are not your personal strength.
3. When working with lower-performing teachers, assess which curriculum areas might cause the most difficulty. Identify these as areas for growth and provide resources for developing richer content understandings.

Knowledge of Teaching Skills and Strategies

Expert teachers, like concert violinists, consciously develop their performance repertoires. They assemble and hone microroutines that combine and apply to fit a wide variety of conditions and settings. Master teachers automatize many routines and basic moves to free cognitive space for more sophisticated sensing of learners' needs. Such unconscious competence is the mark of an expert in the classroom. The lack of automaticity with basic moves, such as getting and maintaining student attention, giving clear directions, and establishing routines for smooth classroom transitions, consumes the emotional and physical energy of novice and low-performing teachers. For this reason, these and other areas of basic classroom management are usually the first level of concerns addressed in supervisory interactions with teachers. Until fundamentals are under control, there is often little space for more sophisticated investigations of instructional practice. Lack of comfort in these arenas blocks a teacher's openness to ideas and resources that address other areas of teaching practice.

Content specific pedagogy is an important variable that increases student success (Sadler et al., 2013; Hill, Rowan & Ball, 2005; Wenglinsky, 2000). Students whose teachers help them to develop higher-order thinking and problem-solving skills linked to specific content areas outperform students whose teachers convey only lower-order skills. Effective supervisors support this essential part of the novice-to-expert journey and often apply a consulting stance when exploring specific teaching techniques.

Section 6: From Novice to Expert Teaching

Pedagogical Content Knowledge

Knowing content and knowing how students learn that content are separate kinds of knowledge. Pedagogical Content Knowledge or PCK (Shulman, 1987) refers to the blend of content knowledge, learner knowledge, and teaching knowledge that connects subject matter to targeted learning strategies. Expert teachers assemble and draw upon a rich collection of analogies, models, memory aids, and explanatory approaches to represent ideas and understandings to their students. They also develop tricks of the trade to help students grapple willingly with misconceptions and to acknowledge them as part of the learning process.

Figure 6.2 Pedagogical Content Knowledge

Effective teachers mesh knowledge and skill sets to produce contextually rich connections for learners. These teachers represent concepts and content through culturally and developmentally appropriate illustrations, examples, explanations, demonstrations, and engaging learning experiences (see Figure 6.2 Pedagogical Content Knowledge). For example, for math instruction, teachers need to be able to calculate correctly and know how to use physical objects, pictures, or diagrams to represent concepts and procedures. These teachers are able to provide students with appropriate explanations for rules and processes. They analyze students' solutions and explanations to inform instruction. When teachers have a clear model of how students learn a specific concept, they can construct learning experiences that help students commit to and test their own ideas. For example, in science instruction, a teacher who knows only the scientific truth appears to have limited effectiveness, particularly if there is a cultural belief that may make acceptance of the scientific view or model difficult.

Implications & Applications: Knowledge of Teaching Skills and Strategies

Implications

Effective classroom practitioners have a well-integrated set of instructional skills, and they draw from a repertoire of instructional strategies to match students' learning needs.

1. What percentage of your supervisory interactions involve supporting teachers with developing and improving fundamental classroom routines and procedures?
2. What are some critical differences between your learning-focused conversations with teachers who have well-run classrooms and those who struggle?

Applications

1. During planning conversations, take a collaborative stance to examine the teaching standards for skillful instruction and choose developmentally appropriate goals for increasing expertise.
2. Create a list of essential instructional skills for well-run classrooms (this could be for grade-level or content area). Use this list as topics for your invitational inquiries during learning-focused conversations. Be prepared to shift stance depending on responses.

Knowledge of Learners and Learning

The greatest teaching repertoire in the world is wasted if it is not well matched to learners' needs (Saphier, Haley-Speca & Gower, 2018). The changing reality in today's classrooms challenges many teachers. The exploding knowledge base about social-emotional learning, cultural and gender identity, and brain development is central to supervisory conversations that focus on producing success for all students.

The push for smaller class sizes and smaller schools is a response to the need to know one another. In an increasingly diverse world, personal knowledge and close relationships connect learners to teachers, to important ideas, and to one another. Teaching students to manage their emotions and behavior and to make meaningful friendships is as important for school success as cognitive and academic skills. These self-regulation capacities are particularly important for students faced with multiple life stressors (Shanker, 2017).

Concerns about student discipline, disaffection, lack of commitment, and alienation from school can test novice and veterans alike. Proactively supporting teachers with managing these aspects of classroom work reduces the overall stress load and frees physical and emotional energy for other important teaching and learning tasks (Zins et al., 2004).

Given an increasingly diverse student population, the need for culturally responsive approaches to teaching and learning looms large. There are significant discrepancies in both learning outcomes and learning conditions for students depending on race, culture, language, socioeconomic status, and learning differences. Further, while the U.S. student population is increasingly diverse, the teaching force remains predominately white middle-class women, which creates a demographic divide (Gay & Howard, 2000). Thus, most teachers do not have the same cultural frames of reference as their students.

Section 6: From Novice to Expert Teaching

The intrinsically sociocultural nature of learning and the importance of connecting prior experience to new information makes it critical that teachers understand students' backgrounds and points of view to structure meaningful learning experiences for all of them (Lipton & Wellman, 2000). Teachers who approach student diversity with a learning mindset can be both academically challenging and culturally responsive to students. This orientation and skill set requires a broad base of knowledge that expands and changes as students, contexts, and content shift. This mindset is an important area to consider in learning-focused conversations.

Materials and methods that are effective for some learners may confuse or repel others. There is an important overlap for teachers between this area and knowledge of self. How a teacher came to know an idea or discipline may not be an appropriate or effective match for the students now learning that same material.

Language differences are emerging as an important variable for teachers to consider. There is a critical variance among students' social discourse and their formal knowledge of the structure and norms of academic discourse in specific content fields (Lee et al., 2008). Skilled teachers help students bridge their own language to formal academic language while integrating personal and cultural relevance with content understandings. This learning is more robust and more likely to be retained. Ultimately, all teachers, no matter their content specialties, are teachers of language and thinking.

Developmental differences extend far beyond the primary grades. Over the years, differences amplify as the cognitive span between students widens. There are many middle- and high-school students who operate at a solid concrete operational level. These learners often run headlong into a curriculum organized by abstractions introduced through symbol systems. When teachers recognize these learning patterns and they approach instruction flexibly, they begin lessons and units with concrete examples, often drawing on students' life experiences. They then help students represent ideas with pictures and graphics as they support student language development and meaning-making. This pathway leads students to firmer conceptual development and richer understandings of abstract ideas and skills integration (Lipton & Wellman, 2000).

> "Ultimately, all teachers, no matter their content specialties, are teachers of language and thinking."

Learning-Focused Supervision

Implications & Applications: Knowledge of Learners and Learning

Implications

Teachers' awareness of their students' cultures and backgrounds allows for building on prior knowledge and experiences, creating relevant examples, and developing productive teaching and learning relationships.

1. In your supervisory conversations, what are some ways you determine the degree to which teachers draw on students' backgrounds when designing and delivering instruction?
2. What are some ways you might increase a teacher's awareness of any mismatches between the relevance of their examples and instructional approaches and student readiness and understanding?

Applications

1. In planning conversations, explore the ways in which the teacher thinks about differentiating instructional approaches, given the composition of the class. Inquire about choice of materials, teaching strategies, and response patterns.
2. During reflecting conversations, use formal and informal assessment results to look for patterns that identify which student groups are succeeding and which are struggling. Explore connections between content knowledge, instructional strategies, and the particular class demographics.

Knowledge of Self

A teaching career is a lifelong journey of professional learning. When supervisors are explicit about this goal, they facilitate a professional vision of the ongoing pursuit of increasing expertise. Knowledge of one's own work-style preferences is a special area of self-knowledge. It is important for teachers to realize that their preferred style may not be that of all of their students. It is also important for supervisors to realize that their own work style may differ from teachers they supervise. Some people perceive and process the world globally. Others prefer more sequential approaches. Some are task driven and others are relationship driven (Lipton & Wellman, 2015). All style preferences, and the many subtle ways they manifest, appear in teaching and supervisory relationships. The ability to stretch against one's preferred work style is a hallmark of the flexibility necessary to connect with a wide variety of learners.

Knowledge of self includes knowledge of the values, beliefs, and personal standards that guide daily decision-making. If teachers are to be effective with an increasingly diverse student population, they need to recognize and understand their own worldview before they can appreciate and honor the worldviews of their students (McAllister & Irvine, 2000). Values and beliefs shape the perceptions and judgments that guide teachers through their days. These values and beliefs undergird both personal and student learning goals. They are the most influential element in the type of classroom culture and

> "The ability to stretch against one's preferred work style is a hallmark of the flexibility necessary to connect with a wide variety of learners."

learning environment that teachers develop with their students (Raths & McAninch, 2003; Pajares, 1992).

Beliefs about the nature of learning and the purposes and processes of teaching influence curricular and instructional approaches. Beliefs shape priorities for what students should learn and what and how to assess. Beliefs and values can also cause conflict between teachers and their colleagues, administrators, and/or parents. Conflicting values include nurturing a child versus pushing for high academic performance; thinking and problem-solving versus success on standardized tests; igniting personal passions versus career readiness; and creating global citizens versus reinforcing local values.

With the press of the clock and calendar, teachers make decisions about what to emphasize and what to let slide. These choices are, at heart, a matter of values and beliefs. Bringing these to conscious attention helps a teacher address conflicting options and the sometimes conflicting goals encountered when personal beliefs and values bump headlong into institutional beliefs and values. Supervisors can help teachers stretch their thinking in this sphere by bringing values and potential conflicts to consciousness as decision-making tools.

Implications & Applications: Knowledge of Self

Implications

Teachers' values, beliefs, and personal standards drive decision-making and influence perceptions, judgments, and choices.

1. What are some of the tensions between your beliefs and values and those of your teachers as related to teaching and learning standards?
2. What are some ways that teachers' clarity about their values and beliefs contributes to having respectful relationships in their classrooms?

Applications

1. Given your understanding of this sphere, make a list of some ways your own self-knowledge influences your classroom observations, conversations, and staff interactions.
2. During learning-focused conversations, consider the elements in this sphere that have the most impact on a teacher's effectiveness (e.g., discipline approaches, curricular prioritizing, lesson and unit design). Construct lines of inquiry related to these areas.

Knowledge of Collaboration

Developing expertise in teaching is a joint venture that requires knowledge of the whys and hows of collaboration. By working in communities of practice, teachers expand and energize their own learning, which positively affects student learning. In powerful professional communities, the work of teaching and the craft knowledge for doing it skillfully are collective property. Productive teacher teams regularly gather evidence of students' products and performances and use the data to evaluate and modify instruction, working together to improve their own and others' instructional skills (Hattie, 2009).

Learning-Focused Supervision

Successful collaboration both requires and develops the knowledge, skills, and dispositions for learning with and from colleagues. This is as true for veterans as it is for beginners. An essential value—and a key component of a professional vision—is that working with others is an important part of a teacher's work, not something that keeps them from their work. In healthy collegial cultures, professionals take responsibility for the learning of all students in the school and understand the links to how their own ways of working drive improvements in student performance. Ongoing cycles of assessment, inquiry, analysis, pattern seeking, and planning provide teachers with a fine-grained sense of the cumulative effects of shared practices (Wellman & Lipton, 2017).

> "In powerful professional communities, the work of teaching and the craft knowledge for doing it skillfully are collective property."

Expert collaborators have practical knowledge about how adults work and learn together in groups. They know how to contribute to others' learning and how to develop ideas and resources with their fellow professionals. Productive peer interaction takes courage, requiring teachers at all levels of experience to negotiate the vulnerabilities and insecurities of opening their physical and metaphorical classroom doors to the scrutiny of others. Structuring and supporting the growth of teachers as collaborative colleagues is a vital supervisory responsibility.

Implications & Applications: Knowledge of Collaboration

Implications

Successful teacher collaboration develops collective expertise and requires the knowledge, skills, and dispositions for learning from and contributing to the learning of others.

1. What are some ways that you model and reinforce the importance of collaboration in your supervisory interactions?
2. What are some indicators that you look for to determine a teacher's level of collaborative skills?

Applications

1. Include professional collaboration skills when setting goals with your teachers. Provide opportunities for achieving these goals (e.g., study groups, data teams, PLCs, etc.). Make time to reflect on these experiences as part of your supervisory conversations.
2. Design staff meetings to include purposeful collaborative interactions to model effective group processes. Reflect on those processes with your staff.

Section 6: From Novice to Expert Teaching

The Transition from Novice to More Expert Teaching

Experience and expertise are not the same thing. Someone can have ten years of classroom experience and still be a mid-level performer. The supervisory challenge is helping teachers recognize this reality and appreciate that running a classroom with minimal disciplinary issues is not the same as managing a vibrant learning environment.

Experts think differently about their practice than novices do. Expert teachers are able to operate both in the moment and over time with clear outcomes in mind, skillfully managing students, content, equipment, materials, the clock, and the calendar. They also apply greater complexity and sophistication to analyzing and understanding instructional problems.

The Inner Voice of Expertise

The self-talk of experts differs greatly from that of novices. Expert teachers develop and internalize patterns and behaviors that free their attention for the more interactive and dynamic needs of classroom practice. Expert teachers automatize routines for management tasks such as taking attendance and focusing students' attention. They have mental scripts for tasks such as monitoring student understanding, varying call-and-response patterns, and dignifying errors and responding to student misconceptions. Automaticity with these procedures and moves frees teachers' mental and physical energy to focus on student learning needs and ways to respond to them (Wiliam, 2016; Berliner, 2001).

Expert teachers access their informed self-talk in a variety of ways, such as monitoring decisions, choices, and the impact of actions. This is the inner voice of expertise. As master teachers access this resource, they continually sort through their internalized knowledge bases about the structure of the discipline they are currently teaching, their instructional repertoire, knowledge of the individual students with whom they are working, and knowledge about their own goals, values, and beliefs (see Five Spheres of Teaching Expertise, p. 103). As they sort this treasure trove of options, master teachers mentally articulate and apply clear criteria for their selections.

The kinds and qualities of filters is what most separates experts from novices. Expert teachers are able to pursue multiple goals for a wider variety of students during the flow of a lesson than novices. Experts always have big-picture outcomes for thinking and social skills, and they continually reinforce them. They manage relationships with the whole class while they intervene and support individual learners. Experts design specific lessons that fit within a bigger curriculum plan that operates all the time. Novices and other teachers on the lower rungs of the developmental ladder tend to be more immediate and intent on managing the flow of a specific lesson plan or controlling student behavior.

Accessing this sophisticated and complex inner voice is the essence of intention-driven action in the classroom. This vital feedback loop helps alert teachers to match their choices and behaviors with their intentions and encourages in-flight reflection and self-monitoring. This attention might mean monitoring the pace of one's speech and use of pauses to elicit student

Learning-Focused Supervision

thinking. It also might mean controlling emotions when responding to a difficult student. In essence, it is the thermostat of self-control that regulates attention, task focus, impulsiveness, humor, and a host of emotional, mental, and physical responses.

When confronting new professional learning challenges, the voice of the skilled supervisor rings loudly in the inner voice of the teacher. As teachers internalize increasingly productive classroom habits, they also learn to listen to and trust their own self-talk.

> **EXPERT MOVE**
>
> Skilled supervisors craft their ideas and questions for ease of transfer to support the development of teacher expertise at early stages. Consistent use of structured conversations helps teachers internalize best practices for planning, reflecting, and problem-solving. A supervisor's choice of language and purposeful use of each stance influences the inner dialogue of teachers as they refine their practice.

Five Stages of Growth

The quest for expertise is a developmental process in all fields. Mastery is a practice that requires practice. Skilled growth agents articulate and model deliberate practice in all disciplines. For example, giving task directions is one chunk for expert teachers. For novices, this act requires multiple conscious elements including focusing attention, pacing of delivery, modulating intonation, choosing appropriate vocabulary, using visuals, and monitoring student understanding. Each of these elements needs to be isolated and deliberately practiced in order to become integrated.

Expert teachers as described above draw upon a wealth of craft knowledge to plan instruction, solve problems, and analyze their effectiveness. This knowledge is not always explicit; in fact, it may be so well integrated that it seems intuitive for skilled veterans. That the primary source for teacher learning is, in fact, their own context and content specific experience may not be very encouraging for those new to an educational practice or struggling to master a new curriculum. However, the internal scripts and routines of experts can be shared and transferred to others when they receive standards-based feedback and refine their criteria for self-assessment.

Craft knowledge and expertise in teaching take time to acquire. For supervisors and teachers alike, it is useful to know that the transition from novice to expert occurs in predictable, measurable stages. David Berliner describes five distinct stages in this journey: novice, advanced beginner, competent, proficient, and expert (Calderhead, 1996).

"Mastery is a practice that requires practice."

Five Stages of Growth

Novice

Novice teachers seek the comfort of rules and procedures for guidance. They seek external guidelines and others' judgments to determine the correctness of their actions. They cling to the comfort of the teacher's guide and ask for validation from supervisors regarding progress. Descriptions become prescriptions, and planning takes the form of preparing the exact lesson presented in the curriculum guide or instructional manual. Initially there is little variation from the scripted text and scant attention to individual student responses. Their lack of repertoire leads them to duplicate the lesson as planned in the precise sequence. They have little capacity for monitoring their class and adjusting the instruction accordingly.

Advanced Beginner

Advanced beginners start to stretch the pattern a bit. They are in the early stages of developing richer knowledge about basic classroom operations, their students, and teaching specific subjects. Their growing knowledge of the curriculum, the classroom, and their content area increases their confidence to flex. They are better able to season the prescribed lesson plans with strategies of their own, and to adjust the lesson based on student responses. They are comfortable incorporating tips from colleagues and supervisors and are forming their own preferences in both content and technique.

Competent

Competent teachers have the ability to read student responses and change course to meet learning needs. They are goal oriented across a spectrum of instructional concerns. They can differentiate instruction both in planning and in implementation. Ongoing assessment of student progress determines lesson design. The teacher's manual no longer controls the instructional decision-making.

Proficient

Proficient teachers incorporate all of the attributes of competency and also hold a much larger picture of practice than teachers at previous stages. They operate at multiple levels simultaneously. They also have a broader temporal horizon and skillfully craft goals and organize instruction for both short-term and long-term gains.

Expert

Expert teachers continue to expand personal and professional proficiency in all areas of their teaching. Automatized routines free attention for richer and more focused interactions with learners. There is an organic flow to their day that extends to the ways students self-manage many classroom routines. Teachers at this stage are proactive and can anticipate and address potential problems before they arise. They have fluidity in applying their wide array of technical knowledge and skills about learning and learners. When problems do emerge, they can generate multiple solutions and make effective choices. They see children as unique individuals and their personal catalog of learner types helps to assemble targeted materials and lessons that smooth learning pathways for all students. Their capacity to generalize from their rich experience guides their decision-making, which enables them to create lessons that target materials and instruction into an organic flow. They cultivate self-managing and self-directed learners.

Learning-Focused Supervision

Supervision Across Developmental Stages

The development from novice to expert takes many years of experience. While a beginner struggles to master basic classroom routines, the effective instructional practices of their more skilled colleagues may seem unattainable. The need for conscious attention to scaffolding teacher learning from practice is one of the gifts of learning-focused supervision.

According to Berliner's research, the novice stage occupies the first year of teaching. Most teachers reach the competence stage after three or four years, with only a modest proportion moving to the proficient stage and fewer still attaining expert status. It is important to note that expertise is context specific. Most teachers show steady improvement in the first few years of practice, and student learning gains are greater when teachers teach the same grade every year (Jacob & Rockoff, 2011). The growth from novice to more expert teaching requires more than simple experience. It is also a highly personal voyage through the seas of professional learning. Having a skilled navigator along to plot the course and find safe harbors increases the safety of the journey and allows one to enjoy the adventure. Skilled supervisors offer a navigational chart, a compass, and markers for the route ahead.

The Five Spheres of Teaching Expertise offer a conceptual framework for interpreting, analyzing, and planning for teachers' professional learning. Below are practical approaches for listening and responding to teachers in ways that match current developmental stages in those five areas and stretch their thinking to next levels of growth.

Developmental Practice: Seven Lenses for Listening

A teacher's developmental stage influences a supervisor's decisions regarding the stance to take with a given instructional issue. In both formal and informal interactions, attentive supervisors pay attention to teachers' language as a way to gain insight into their current inner voices. They note how a teacher thinks about their content, student goals, instructional strategies, potential choice points, use of data, problem-solving, and collaborative practices with colleagues (see Table 6.1 Seven Lenses for Listening).

Understanding the levels of emerging expertise is an essential source for identifying developmental supervisory approaches. Mindful supervisors structure interactions that match and then stretch teachers' current knowledge and skills. Asking teachers questions that are too far beyond their ability may be detrimental to their confidence and to the supervisory relationship. The following seven lenses for listening provide information for growth-oriented supervisors regarding a teacher's current level of development (see Table 6.1 Seven Lenses for Listening). By employing these perspectives, supervisors can plan strategies to serve learning needs in the moment and over time.

Section 6: From Novice to Expert Teaching

Table 6.1 Seven Lenses for Listening

Learning-Focused Supervisors Attend to:	Novice	Emerging Competence	Expert
Depth of Content Knowledge	Focused on coverage	Provides vivid, culturally appropriate examples Maintains flexibility by sorting nice from necessary	Connects and interweaves concepts and big ideas Models discipline-based thinking
Source of Goals for Lessons and Units	Over-reliance on external sources: learning standards, curriculum documents, teacher's guides	Expands beyond content objectives to integrate cognitive and social-emotional outcomes Establishes both short- and long-term goals	Derived from an understanding of content matched to individual and collective student learning needs Targeted towards self-managing, self-directed learners
Instructional Design and Delivery	Activity-based planning Does not deviate from plan during teaching	Strategies are goal-driven, informed by informal and formal assessments, and customized and differentiated to meet student needs	Applies a rich repertoire of instructional scaffolds, analogies, models, and memory aids
Ability to Recognize and Generate Choice Points	Unaware that there are choice points in lessons Sticks to the plan, watches the clock	Envisions success indicators Plans for what-ifs Frequently checks for understanding	Multidimensional, in-flight adjustments Wide repertoire of go-tos Seizes the teachable moment: for the class, small groups, and individual students
Depth of Evidence Cited	Data collection is not built into plans Taps limited sources of data	Applies multiple measures Assessment-driven planning	Wide range of data types and sources Searches for patterns
Approaches to Problem-Solving	Focused on immediate solutions Seeks advice: "Tell me what to do"	Frames problems before developing solutions	Takes a balcony view to gain perspective Frames and reframes problems Generates multiple possible solutions
Relationship to Professional Community	Fearful of self-disclosure Consumes more than contributes	Sees collaboration as part of professional responsibilities Draws from and contributes to colleagues' thinking	Promotes collective responsibility for student learning Commits to group's goals and growth

The following pages illustrate Supervisor Strategies for each of the Seven Lenses for Listening.

Learning-Focused Supervision

The Depth of Content Knowledge

Expert practitioners have deep knowledge of the structure of the discipline, or disciplines, they teach. They can sort the nice from the necessary when developing and applying curricular outcomes to daily instruction. They make critical choices when time is short regarding these distinctions. Lesson plans demonstrate a relationship between what has already been learned and what is expected in future lessons. Skillful teachers also know where to emphasize important and recurring concepts that are foundational to further learning. Expertise in this area includes the ability to articulate connections between large ideas in the curriculum and to support students in making those connections.

As supervisors attend fully during their conversations, they listen to determine the degree that a teacher does the following things:

- Understands the knowledge, skills, and concepts in a lesson or unit
- Articulates the connections among ideas in the curriculum
- Employs culturally relevant examples to illustrate the content/concepts
- Recognizes the place of a specific lesson/unit in the larger frame of the curriculum
- Describes the thinking habits within a discipline

Table 6.2 Supervisor Strategies for Developing Depth of Content Knowledge

The teacher focuses on coverage and replicates lesson plans from the teacher's guide; there is a lack of connection between big ideas and limited use of examples to illuminate content.		
Supervisor Strategy	What is it?	What it might look/sound like
Ask a coaching question	A question designed to support connection-making between pieces of content and increase awareness of students' relationship to the content that also provides an assessment for the supervisor	*"In this lesson, what are the most critical content understandings you want to get across?"* or *"What are some connections between the content of this lesson and the larger concepts of the unit?"* or *"Given your experience with this grade level, what are some examples that might make this content real for your kids?"*
Provide a what, why, and how for relevant examples followed by a shift to a collaborating stance	A consulting strategy that offers ideas and the rationale for ideas, which prime the pump for co-generation	*"For your unit on simple machines, you can bring in pictures of household items such as levers, pulleys, wedges, and so on. This is important because providing concrete examples that students can relate to increases understanding and retention. You might do this with an online image search, or a kitchen supply catalog and some cutting and pasting. The cards could then be used for a sorting and classifying activity or a matching game. Let's consider that as a starter and generate some additional examples for later in the unit."*
Use content standards as a third point, calibrate to the standard, and then shift to a coaching stance and inquire	A way to clarify the expected standard with specific examples and to inquire to support more expert thinking about achieving the standard	*"At this grade level, students are expected to understand the connections between simple machines and the concepts of force, motion, and work. The big idea is that simple machines conserve human energy and make work easier. What are some ways this standard relates to what you've already taught and where you're headed?"*

Section 6: From Novice to Expert Teaching

The Source of Goals for Lessons and Units

As expertise develops, teachers move from strict adherence to the teacher's guide or other external sources, to their own understanding of the content and students' needs to determine learning goals. The confident marriage of learning standards to source materials when goal setting is a developmental indicator. In addition, setting learning goals that nest short-term objectives within longer-term outcomes and connecting the specific lesson or unit to the broader conceptual understandings of the curriculum or content area are indicators of growing expertise. So too are goals that include specific thinking skills or clusters of thinking skills, such as problem-solving or decision-making, and social skills such as listening to other points of view or engaging productively in a group task.

As supervisors attend fully in conversations, they listen to determine to what degree the teacher does the following things:

- References curriculum guides and learning standards to set goals
- Sets both group and individual goals
- Sets and manages both short- and long-term goals
- Integrates content goals with social-emotional and cognitive goals

Table 6.3 Supervisor Strategies for Developing the Source of Goals for Lessons and Units

The teacher focuses on content goals primarily from external sources.		
Supervisor Strategy	What is it?	What it might look/sound like
Ask a coaching question	A question designed to expand the sources for goal setting and increase the integration of other types of goals (e.g., social-emotional or cognitive processes)	*"In addition to the content objectives, what other outcomes might be important for your students to take away from this lesson?"* or *"What are some ways your approach to this unit fits into your social-emotional outcome goals for this semester?"*
Offer a principle of practice, then shift to a collaborating stance	A consulting strategy that provides the conceptual "why" that is a basis for stimulating collaborative thinking	*"It's important that goals target both short- and long-term outcomes. Let's think about a sequence for learning goals in this upcoming unit."*
Use curriculum documents as a third point, calibrate to the unit goals, and then shift to a coaching stance and inquire	A way to illustrate and clarify that content goals connect to overarching learning outcomes and to provide specific examples and inquire to support more expert thinking about developing integrated goals	*"Notice that in this reading lesson, the content goal is about characterization, and the thinking skill goals include compare/contrast and inferential reasoning."* and *"As you think about upcoming lessons and other units, how might you integrate these fundamental thinking skills?"*

Learning-Focused Supervision

Instructional Design and Delivery

Designing strategies to meet specific outcomes and modifying them to differentiate for individual learners is an expert skill. A mindful supervisor listens to determine whether the teacher is applying instructional methods strategically, or simply doing activity thinking. The former is a purposeful application, based on the assessment of learner needs, while the latter is often something found in a teaching journal, sourcebook, or the classroom next door that seems interesting.

As supervisors attend fully in conversations, they listen to determine to what degree the teacher does the following things:

- Draws on a rich repertoire of instructional strategies
- Has clear criteria for choosing instructional strategies
- Customizes and differentiates chosen strategies

Table 6.4 Supervisor Strategies for Developing Instructional Design and Delivery

The teacher engages in activity-based planning and does not adjust instruction based on student responses.		
Supervisor Strategy	What is it?	What it might look/sound like
Ask a coaching question	A question designed to highlight the relationship between the choice of strategy and the learning goal or goals and student readiness	"Given what you know about your students at this point, how will this strategy build on their present skills?" or "What are some criteria you use to determine which instructional strategies will be most effective?"
Think aloud about how you match strategies to goals, and then shift to a collaborative stance to co-generate additional criteria for choosing instructional strategies	Modeling an expert's self-talk regarding instructional design and highlighting the need for criteria-based planning	"When I think about strategy choice, one important element is student learning goals. So I would mentally scan for options, then consider student-learning goals and readiness to find the best match. Let's brainstorm additional criteria that make sense to you for strategy choice."
Reference a standard for effective planning as a third point and calibrate to the rubric descriptions, such as effective use of materials and resources, then shift to a coaching stance and inquire	A way to clarify a standard with context specific examples, then inquire to expand the teacher's thinking about effective implementation of the standard, then inquire to expand the teacher's thinking about criteria for choosing strategies	"As the standard indicates, instructional materials and strategies need to appropriately match the learning needs of your students. Based on your sense of student readiness, what are some ways you determine strategy choice?"

Section 6: From Novice to Expert Teaching

The Ability to Recognize and Generate Choice Points

For skillful teachers, clear intentions regarding learning outcomes drive instructional choices. As proactive planners, these teachers incorporate if/then thinking to build potential contingencies into a lesson or unit of study. When implementing planned choices, including instructional objectives, learning materials, interaction and grouping patterns, and time management, these teachers consistently monitor their effectiveness. They make adjustments to meet the immediate needs of the learners, while being mindful of the larger instructional picture. The ability to draw from repertoire to make in-the-moment refinements or revisions to the initial plan is a hallmark of expertise.

As supervisors attend fully in conversations, they listen to determine to what degree the teacher does the following things:

- Describes the need to modify instruction based on observations of student behavior
- Considers what-ifs during planning processes
- Embeds checks for understanding in lesson plans

Table 6.5 Supervisor Strategies for Developing Ability to Recognize and Generate Choice Points

The teacher identifies limited options for choice while planning or teaching and is not consistent about checking for understanding during lessons.		
Supervisor Strategy	What is it?	What it might look/sound like
Ask a coaching question	A question designed to increase awareness of the need to anticipate choice points	"As you think about teaching this lesson, where are some places you anticipate the need for a plan B?" or "Imagine your students are meeting your expectations, what might be some ways to seize that moment and build on their success?"
Offer a menu and then shift to a collaborating stance	A consulting strategy that expands instructional repertoire and offers potential options that establishes readiness for co-determining pros and cons of each one	"Given the need to determine whether you need to modify your plan, there are several ways you might check for students' understanding in this math lesson: a signal like thumbs up/down, ask a question and randomly select responders, or have students write a response and hold up mini whiteboards. Let's consider the pros and cons of these techniques based on what you know about your students."
Use the teaching standard for effective instruction as a third point and calibrate to the rubric descriptions, such as adjusting the lesson based on student responses; then shift to a coaching stance and inquire	A way to clarify a standard with context specific examples, then inquire to expand the teacher's thinking about effective implementation of the standard, then inquire to develop increased awareness regarding flexibility and responsiveness before and during instruction	"This standard is based on the need to be poised to modify a plan at any point and to be a proactive planner for that contingency. What are some ways that you determine whether students are with you or if you need to flex?"

Learning-Focused Supervision

Depth of Evidence Cited

Effective teaching requires the application of day-to-day and moment-to-moment assessment of student learning to inform future action. Expert teachers draw upon a wide range of data sources for planning and reflecting on learning. Possibilities include text-based inventories, student work products, teacher-made tests, classroom observation of student behaviors, learner interviews, and inventories, all of which are rich resources for determining short- and long-term next steps for individual students, groups of students, and the class as a whole.

As supervisors attend fully in conversations, they listen to determine to what degree the teacher does the following things:

- Draws on multiple measures to determine student progress
- Engages in assessment driven planning and reflecting
- Builds data collection into lesson plans
- Searches for and acts upon patterns in the data

Table 6.6 Supervisor Strategies for Developing Depth of Evidence Cited

The teacher taps limited sources of data to guide planning and instructional decision-making.		
Supervisor Strategy	What is it?	What it might look/sound like
Ask a coaching question	A question designed to increase awareness about assessment driven planning and reflecting, and to increase the repertoire of options for formative and summative assessments	"What methods for determining student progress are you building into this lesson?" or "Given the student work you've collected and your in-class observations, what's your degree of confidence in student progress on a scale of 1 to 5?"
Refer to research regarding formative assessment, and shift to a collaborating stance to co-design applications	A consulting strategy that presents a research-based rationale for effective action and sets the stage for collaboratively generating practical ways to apply these findings	"Current research indicates that formative assessment is one of the most powerful influences on student learning success. Frequent checks for understanding are an important part of this process. Let's design some formative assessments for your next lesson."
Use the standard on using assessment in instruction as a third point, calibrate to the rubric descriptions then shift to a coaching stance and inquire	A way to clarify a standard with context specific examples, then inquire to expand the teacher's thinking about ways to monitor student learning	"This standard addresses the importance of continuous monitoring of student learning. In your class, that would mean identifying the types of data that would most help you determine learning successes and challenges for all students. Given these criteria, what might be some ways to gather formative assessment information using student work products in your upcoming lessons?"

Section 6: From Novice to Expert Teaching

Approaches to Problem-Solving

Expert problem-solvers spend the bulk of their energy defining the problem before seeking solutions. They understand that both problem definition and clear success indicators set the direction for productive resolution. Expert problem-solvers can step outside of the immediate situation to access emotional resourcefulness, gain perspective on patterns and causal factors, and seek multiple solutions. These capacities contribute to their confidence and ability to effectively resolve challenging issues.

As supervisors attend fully in conversations, they listen to determine to what degree the teacher does the following things:

- Searches for patterns to better understand the issue
- Considers multiple causal factors to define problems
- Engages in problem-framing/reframing before developing solutions

Table 6.7 Supervisor Strategies for Developing Approaches to Problem-Solving

The teacher seeks quick solutions (often from others) before defining the problem.		
Supervisor Strategy	What is it?	What it might look/sound like
Ask a coaching question	A question designed to shift the teacher's energy to define the problem before generating solutions	*"What's your hunch about what might be triggering these behaviors?"* or *"What are some patterns you notice when these behaviors occur?"*
Offer potential causal factors and then shift to a collaborating stance	A consulting strategy that shifts energy to problem causes rather than problem fixes and provides a context for a paired conversation about the most likely causes prior to seeking solutions	*"So you're finding that many of your students can't accurately measure materials in your chemistry labs. Some possible factors that might be causing this problem are not knowing how to read the scales, not correctly transferring their readings to the lab sheets, or not understanding why accuracy matters. Let's consider which of these, if any, are the most likely causes."*
Offer a principle of practice related to expert problem-solving and inquire to determine the scope and scale of the problem	A way to name the importance of problem-framing prior to seeking solutions and then offer a question intended to determine how the teacher is presently considering the issue and to gather more specific information about the parameters	*"Carefully defining the problem before rushing to solutions is one hallmark of successful problem-solving."* and *"When you say accurate measurement, what percentage of your students are struggling with this skill?"*

Relationship to Professional Community

Being a contributing member of a vital learning community is an important professional responsibility. Teachers who seek collaboration and draw from and contribute to their colleagues' thinking are valued members of a learning culture. These teachers are committed to the group's goals, share responsibility for all students' learning, and identify themselves as part of a group that is continuously improving.

As supervisors attend fully in conversations, they listen to determine to what degree the teacher does the following things:

- Engages in collaborative activities
- Draws from and contributes to colleagues' thinking
- Expresses commitment to the group's goals and growth
- Shares responsibility for all students' learning

Table 6.8 Supervisor Strategies for Developing Relationship to Professional Community

The teacher expresses concern about ways to participate in team meetings, seems fearful of self-disclosure, and limits participation in collaborative activities.		
Supervisor Strategy	**What is it?**	**What it might look/sound like**
Ask a coaching question	A question designed to increase the teacher's value for being a participating team member	"What are some things you notice about your participation as a team member?" or "What are some ways you might benefit from engaging in more collaborative activities?"
Offer a perspective shift related to teamwork and then shift to a collaborative stance	A consulting strategy that offers another way of thinking about working as a team member that leads to a shared exploration of both the challenges and rewards of professional community	"It's possible that your colleagues don't want to put any pressure on you, so they carry most of the weight in team meetings. Let's brainstorm some ways you might indicate your interest and readiness for greater participation."
Reference a teaching standard about professional community as a third point, calibrate to the rubric descriptions and then shift to a coaching stance and inquire	A way to clarify a standard with context specific examples, then inquire to increase the teacher's confidence in participating more fully as a team member	"The standard for high performance as a team member describes the importance of contributing to the shared work of improving practice. When you think of opportunities to do that with your team, what are some things that come to mind?"

Teaching expertise does not emerge spontaneously, nor does it transfer by osmosis from one classroom to the next. It is essential for learning-focused supervisors to understand the pathways from novice to more expert teaching and to hone their skills for supporting this journey. The Four Qualities of Learning-Focused Supervision described in Section One frame the key dispositions that guide this process.

Section 6: From Novice to Expert Teaching

All teachers, no matter their current stage of development, have the potential to increase their skills. The growing body of work on teaching expertise offers both goals and entry points for enriching the working relationship between supervisors and teachers.

Supervisory Expertise That Supports Teaching Expertise

Mastering the art and craft of teaching is an unending pursuit for committed professionals. Focused curiosity and a disposition for inquiry about how students learn essential content and skills are the hallmarks of dedicated teachers.

These same attitudes motivate growth-oriented supervisors to hone their skills consciously and persistently to support teacher learning. The Four Qualities of Learning-focused Supervision, The Continuum of Learning-focused Interaction, the templates for structured conversations, and the Learning-focused Tool Kit presented in this volume offer both a schema and a curriculum for the supervisory learning journey. Mastery of the craft of supervision, like any other human endeavor, requires practice, patience with the learning process, and feedback from thoughtful colleagues.

Caring supervisors will always encounter new challenges in their work. Embracing the mindsets and mastering the skills of Learning-focused Supervision increases the confidence and adaptability for seizing these issues as opportunities to promote more learning-focused cultures in their schools.

"Mastery of the craft of supervision, like any other human endeavor, requires practice, patience with the learning process, and feedback from thoughtful colleagues."

Notes · Insights · Applications

References

Bandler, R. & Grinder, J. (1971). *The Structure of Magic: A Book About Language and Therapy.* Palo Alto, CA: Science and Behavior Books.

Berliner, D. (2001). "Learning About and Learning from Expert Teachers." *International Journal of Educational Research,* 35(5): 463–482.

Butt, G. (2008) *Lesson Planning* (3rd Ed.). New York: Continuum International Publishing Group.

Calderhead, J. (1996). "Teachers: Beliefs and Knowledge." In D. Berliner & R. C. Calfee (Eds.) *Handbook of Educational Psychology,* 709–725. New York: Routledge.

Carlson, W. S. (1993). "Teacher Knowledge and Discourse Control: Quantitative Evidence from Novice Biology Teachers' Classrooms." *Journal of Research in Science Teaching,* 30(5), 471–481.

Carter, P. & Welner, K. (Eds.) (2013). *Closing the Opportunity Gap: What America Must Do to Give Every Child an Even Chance.* Oxford: Oxford University Press.

Costa, A. & Garmston, R. (2016). *Cognitive Coaching: Developing Self-Directed Leaders and Learners* (3rd Ed.). Lanham, MD: Rowman & Littlefield.

Coyle, D. (2009). *The Talent Code: Greatness Isn't Born. It's Grown. Here's How.* New York: Bantam Books.

Darling-Hammond, L. & Bransford, J. (2005). *Preparing Teachers for a Changing World: What Teachers Should Learn and Be Able to Do.* San Francisco: Jossey-Bass.

Darling-Hammond, L. & Oakes, J. (2019). *Preparing Teachers for Deeper Learning.* Cambridge, MA: Harvard Education Press.

Duhigg, C. (2012). *The Power of Habit: Why We Do What We Do in Life and Business.* New York: Random House.

Edmondson, A., Boyatzis, R., Schaninger, B. (July, 2020). Psychological Safety, Emotional Intelligence, and Leadership In a Time of Flux. McKinsey Quarterly online. https://www.mckinsey.com/featured-insights/leadership/psychological-safety-emotional-intelligence-and-leadership-in-a-time-of-flux

Elgin, S. (2000). *The gentle art of verbal self-defense.* New York: Prentice Hall.

Fisher, D. & Frey, N. (2007). "Implementing a Schoolwide Literacy Framework: Improving Achievement in an Urban Elementary School." *The Reading Teacher,* 61(1), 32–43.

Gay, G. & Howard, T. (2000). "Multicultural Teacher Education for the 21st century." *Teacher Education,* 53(2), 106116.

Goldhaber, D. (2016). "In Schools, Teacher Quality Matters Most." *Education Next,* 16(2), 56–62.

Grinder, M. (1997). *ENVoY: A Personal Guide to Classroom Management*. Battleground, WA: Michael Grinder & Associates.

Grinder, M. (2006). *Charisma: The Art of Relationships*. Battleground, WA: Michael Grinder & Associates.

Hatano, G. & Inagaki, K. (1986). "Two Courses of Expertise." In H. Stevenson, J. Azuma & K. Haguta (Eds.) *Child Development and Education in Japan*, 258–288. New York: W. H. Freeman & Co.

Hattie, J. (2009). *Visible Learning: A Synthesis of Over 800 Meta-Analyses Relating to Achievement*. New York: Routledge.

Hayakawa, S. I. (1964). *Language in Thought and Action*. New York: Harcourt, Brace & World.

Hill, H., Rowan, B. & Ball, D. (2005). "Effects of Teachers' Mathematical Knowledge for Teaching on Student Achievement." *American Educational Research Journal*, 42(2), 371–406.

Ingersoll, R., Merrill, E., Stuckey, D. & Collins, G. (2018). "Seven Trends: The Transformation of the Teaching Force." *Research Report* (#RR 2018-2). Consortium for Policy Research in Education, University of Pennsylvania.

Jacob, B. & Rockoff, J. (2011). "Organizing Schools to Improve Student Achievement: Start Times, Grade Configurations, and Teacher Assignments." *The Hamilton Project research paper* 2011-08. Washington, DC: Brookings Institution.

Klinger, A. (June, 2020). Navigating School Leadership in a Post-Pandemic World. https://www.ascd.org/el/articles/navigating-school-leadership-in-a-post-pandemic-world

Kluger, A. N. & DeNisi, A. (1996). "The Effects of Feedback Interventions on Performance: A Historical Review, a Meta-Analysis, and a Preliminary Feedback Intervention Theory." *Psychological Bulletin*, 119(2), 254–284.

Kini, T. & Podolsky, A. (2016). *Does Teaching Experience Increase Teacher Effectiveness? A Review of the Research*. Palo Alto, CA: Learning Policy Institute.

Kraft, M. & Christian, A. (2019). "In Search of High-Quality Evaluation Feedback: An Administrator Training Field Experiment." (EdWorkingPaper No. 19-62). Providence, RI: Annenberg Institute at Brown University.

Korzybski, A. (1958). *Science and Sanity: An Introduction to Non-Aristotelian Systems and General Semantics*. Brooklyn, NY: Institute of General Semantics.

Lee, O., Maerten-Rivera, J., Penfield, R., LeRoy, K. & Secada, W. (2008). "Science Achievement of English Language Learners in Urban Elementary Schools: Results of a First-Year Professional Development Intervention." *Journal of Research in Science Teaching*, 45(1), 31–52.

Lipton, L. & Wellman, B. (2000). *Pathways to Understanding: Patterns and Practices in the Learning-focused Classroom*. Burlington, VT: MiraVia, LLC.

Lipton, L. & Wellman, B. (2015). *Leading Groups: Effective Strategies for Building Professional Community*. Burlington VT: MiraVia, LLC.

Marzano, R., Pickering D. & Pollack, E. (2001). *Classroom Instruction That Works: Research-Based Strategies for Increasing Student Achievement.* Alexandria, VA: Association for Supervision and Curriculum Development.

McAllister, G. & Irvine, J. J. (2000). "Cross Cultural Competency and Multicultural Teacher Education." *Review of Educational Research,* 70(1), 3–24.

Merseth, K., Cooper, K., Roberts, J., Tieken, M., Valant, J. & Wynne, C. (2009). *Inside Urban Charter Schools: Promising Practices in Five High-Performing Schools.* Cambridge, MA: Harvard Education Press.

National Academies of Sciences, Engineering, and Medicine; Division of Behavioral and Social Sciences and Education; Board on Behavioral, Cognitive, and Sensory Sciences; Board on Science Education; Committee on How People Learn II: The Science and Practice of Learning. (2018). *How People Learn II: Learners, Contexts, and Cultures.* Washington, DC. The National Academies Press.

National Center for Education Statistics, US Department of Education. "The Condition of Education 2018," NCES 2018-144. https://nces.ed.gov/pubs2018/2018144.pdf

National Center for Education Statistics. "Fast Facts: Back to Schools Statistics." US Department of Education.

Pajares, M. F. (1992). "Teachers' Beliefs and Educational Research: Cleaning Up a Messy Construct." *Review of Educational Research,* 62(3), 307–332.

Raths, J. & McAninch, A. C. (Eds.) (2003). *Teacher Beliefs and Classroom Performance: The Impact of Teacher Education.* Greenwich, CT: Information Age Publishing.

Rizzolatti, G. & Arib, M. (1998). "Language Within Our Grasp." *Trends in Neuroscience,* 22(4):151–2.

Rothman, R. (2009). "Behind the Classroom Door." *Harvard Education Letter,* 25(6).

Rowe, M. B. (1986). "Wait-Time: Slowing Down May Be a Way of Speeding Up!" *Journal of Teacher Education,* 37(1), 43–50.

Sadler, P., Sonnert, G., Coyle, H., Cook-Smith, N. & Miller, J. (2013). "The Influence of Teachers' Knowledge on Student Learning in Middle School Physical Science Classrooms." *American Education Research Journal,* 50(8), 1020–1049.

Saphier, J., Haley-Speca, M. & Gower, R. (2018). *The Skillful Teacher: The Comprehensive Resource of Improving Teaching and Learning.* Acton, MA: Research for Better Teaching.

Sartain, L., Stoelinga, S. & Brown, E., with Luppescu, S., Matsko, K., Miller, F., Durwood, C.Jiang, J. & Glazer, D. (2011). "Rethinking Teacher Evaluation in Chicago: Lessons Learned from Classroom Observations, Principal and Teacher Conferences, and District Implementation." Chicago: Consortium on Chicago School Research at the University of Chicago.

Shanker, S. (2017). *Self-Reg: How to Help your Child (and You) Break the Stress Cycle and Successfully Engage with Life.* New York: Penguin Books.

Shulman, L. S. (1987). "Knowledge and Teaching: Foundations of the New Reform." *Harvard Educational Review,* 57(1), 1–22.

Snow, C., Griffin, P. & Burns, M. (Eds.) (2005). *Knowledge to Support the Teaching of Reading: Preparing Teachers for a Changing World.* San Francisco: Jossey-Bass.

Stone, D. & Heen, S. (2014). *Thanks for the Feedback: The Science and Art of Receiving Feedback Well.* New York: Viking.

Sweller, J. (1988). "Cognitive Load During Problem Solving: Effects on Learning." *Cognitive Science,* 12, 257–285.

Taylor, E. & Tyler, J. (2012). "The Effect of Evaluation on Teacher Performance." *American Economic Review,* 102(7), 3626–3651.

Waks, L. (2010). "Two Types of Interpersonal Listening." *Teachers College Record,* 112(11), 2743–2762.

Wellman, B. & Lipton, L. (2017). *Data-Driven Dialogue: A Facilitator's Guide to Collaborative Inquiry.* Burlington, VT: MiraVia LLC.

Wenglinsky, H. (2000). *How Teaching Matters: Bringing the Classroom Back Into Discussions of Teacher Quality.* Princeton, NJ: Educational Testing Service.

Wiggins, G. & McTighe, J. (2005). *Understanding by Design* (2nd ed.). Alexandria, VA: Association for Supervision and Curriculum Development.

Wiliam, D. (2016). *Leadership for Teacher Learning: Creating a Culture Where All Teachers Improve So That All Students Succeed.* West Palm Beach, FL: Learning Sciences International.

Wood, W. (2019). *Good Habits, Bad Habits: The Science of Making Positive Changes That Stick.* New York: Farrar, Straus, and Giroux.

Zins, J., Bloodworth, M., Weissberg, R. & Walberg, H. (2004). "The Scientific Base Linking Social and Emotional Learning to School Success." In J. Zins, R. Weissberg, M. Wang & H. Walberg (Eds.). *Building Academic Success on Social and Emotional Learning: What Does the Research Say?,* 191–210. New York: Teachers College Press.

Index

A

Abstraction
  ladder of 71
  levels of 66-71, 83
  shifting down 68, 67
  shifting up 68, 67
Alignment 60
  physical 55, 59
  vocal 59
Assumptions 1, 81, 88
  Informing Learning-Focused Supervision 1
Attention
  attending fully 55, 58, 60, 69, 82, 85
  communicating attention 59
Attitude and Aptitude 33, 34
Attunement 58, 59, 60
Avoiding bias 88, 89

B

Berliner, David 113, 114, 116
Bias, avoiding 88, 89
Blocks to Understanding
  certainty listening
  detail listening
  personal listening
  predictive listening
Breaking the Habit Cycle

C

Calibrating 11, 13-17, 26-28, 30, 32, 35, 42, 43, 75, 91, 92
Coaching 11, 22, 24-30, 37, 51-53, 75, 91, 92, 98, 118-124
Cognitive load theory 90
Collaborating 11, 21-23, 26-30, 32, 36, 50, 51, 75, 92, 98, 118-124
Components of Inquiry 74

Consulting 11, 17-22, 26-30, 32, 34, 35, 37, 43, 47, 49, 50-53, 75, 91, 92, 98, 118-124
Continuum of Learning-Focused Interaction 11, 27
Conversation(s)
  applying data 91, 92
  customized 33
  goal-setting 47
  structured 41-54, 95
  templates 51-54
    planning 44
    navigating 51
    problem-solving 46
    reflecting 45
Costa, Arthur 24
Covey, Stephen 57
Craft knowledge 17, 102-105, 111, 112, 114
Cueing Stance 26

D

Data
  choosing 90
  standards, and 87
Deliberate Practice 58, 102, 114
DeNisi, Angelo 42
Duhigg, Charles 57

E

Ericsson, Anders iii
Evaluation
  high-quality systems xi
Expertise
  adaptive 101-103
  and the brain 101
  routine 101, 102

Index *(continued)*

F

Feedback
  intervention theory 42
  loops 58, 96, 113
Five Spheres of Teaching Expertise
  knowledge of collaboration 111
  knowledge of learners and
    learning 108
  knowledge of self 110
  knowledge of the structure
    of the discipline 104
  knowledge of teaching skills
    and strategies 106
Five stages of growth 114, 115
Four Qualities of Learning-Focused
  Supervision 5, 6
    developmental 6
    standards-driven 7
    data-based 8
    customized 8
Four Stances: The Continuum of
  Learning-Focused Interaction 11-40
    calibrating 13-16
    collaborating 21-23
    consulting 17-21
    coaching 24-26

G

Garmston, Robert 24
Gesture
  marker 70
  paraphrase, with 70
Goal-Setting
  conversations 47
  equity and excellence, for xii
Growth, five stages of 114, 115
Grinder, Michael 31, 75, 79, 102

H

Habit Cycle 57, 62
Hayakawa, S.I. 71
High-quality evaluation systems xi

I

Inquiry
  components of 74
  invitational 72
  template 86
Intention-driven action
Invitation, components of 74, 75
  approachable voice 75
  attending fully 75
  exploratory language 75
  nondichotomous forms 76
  plural forms 75
  positive presuppositions 76

K

Kluger, Avraham 42
Korzybski, Alfred 78

L

Ladder of Abstraction 71
Language
  marker 70
  vague 82
Listening
  to understand 60-63
  rates 61

M

Marker gesture 70
Marker language 70
Maslow, Abraham xv

N

Navigating
  Continuum of Learning-Focused
    Interaction 29, 30
  conversation templates 51
  strategically 28
Novice to expert 101-126

Index (continued)

P

Paraphrasing
  acknowledge and clarify 66, 68
  gestures with 70
  goal paraphrase 50, 69
  habit, as a 68
  problem-solving, and 68
  shifting level of abstraction 67, 68
  summarizing and organizing
Pathways Learning Model 41
Pausing 64
Pedagogical Content Knowledge 107
Physical referencing 70
Planning
  conversations 43
  templates 44-46
Problem-Solving
  approaches to 123
  conversations 49, 68, 69
  conversation template 46

Q

Questions
  Designing to Promote Thinking 73
  Intention driven 77, 78

R

Reflecting
  conversations 48, 49
  template 45
Rowe, Mary Budd 64

S

Self-assessment
  Primary Trait x, 85
Seven Lenses for Listening 116
  Ability to recognize and
    generate choice points 121
  Approaches to
    problem-solving 123
  Depth of content knowledge 118
  Depth of evidence cited 122

Instructional design
    and delivery 120
  Relationship to professional
    community 124
  Source of goals for lessons
    and units 119
Speaking rate 61
Stages of growth 114, 115
Stance 26-28
  adjusting 28
  cueing 26
Structured conversations 41-54, 95
Supervisory Competencies 12
  Fluency 12
  Flexibility 12
  Fluidity 12

T

Teaching
  expertise, five spheres 103
    knowledge of
      collaboration 111
    knowledge of learners
      and learning 108
    knowledge of self 110
    knowledge of the structure
      of the discipline 104
    knowledge of teaching skills
      and strategies 106
  transition from novice
    to expert 113
  trends in xiii
Templates
  inquiry 86
  planning conversations 44
  problem-solving conversations 46
  reflecting conversations 45
Third point 31-33, 92
Thinking, Stimulating and
  Clarifying 77
Threat detection 58

Index *(continued)*

U

Understanding, Blocks to 61
   certainty listening 62
   detail listening 61
   personal listening 61
   predictive listening 61

V

Vague language, clarifying 82
Verbal and nonverbal
   referencing 70
Video
   as a data source 95
   resources x

W

Wait time 64

About the Authors

Laura Lipton, Ed.D

Laura Lipton is Director of MiraVia, LLC and is an international consultant whose writing, research, keynotes, and seminars focus on effective and innovative instructional practices and on building professional and organizational capacities for enhanced learning. Laura engages with school districts, public and independent schools, departments of education, and international agencies designing and conducting workshops on organizational and group development, learning-focused instruction, literacy development, and growth oriented supervisory and mentoring practices. She applies her extensive experience with professional learning to workshops and seminars conducted globally on topics including learning-focused relationships, data-driven dialogue, teacher leadership, building professional community, developing high-performing teams, action research, and learning-focused mentoring.

Laura is author and co-author of numerous publications related to organizational and professional development. Laura considers her experience orchestrating an open classroom for first/second graders, directing a K-12 Reading Lab, and providing Related Academics on a large vocational education high school campus to be among the highlights of her professional career. Presently, she lives in Burlington, a vibrant university town in Northern Vermont.

Bruce Wellman, M.Ed

Bruce Wellman is an award-winning writer whose work has been honored by the Education Writers Association and the National Staff Development Council. He is the author and co-author of numerous publications related to organization and professional development, mentoring, quality teaching, and improving professional cultures. He has served as a classroom teacher, curriculum coordinator, and staff developer in the Oberlin, Ohio and Concord, Massachusetts public schools. He holds a B.A. degree from Antioch College and a M.Ed. from Lesley College. Bruce and his wife Leslie enjoy living up a dirt road in Southern Vermont, where they enjoy natural history, birdwatching, and nature photography.

Global PD teams
Collaborative Learning for School Improvement

Quality team learning **from authors you trust**

Global PD Teams is the first-ever **online professional development resource designed to support your entire faculty on your learning journey.** This convenient tool offers daily access to videos, mini-courses, eBooks, articles, and more packed with insights and research-backed strategies you can use immediately.

GET STARTED
SolutionTree.com/**GlobalPDTeams**
800.733.6786